About the Author

PHIL O'BRIEN spent his early years on a remote cattle station in the Northern Territory. But a severe drought brought him and his family down to Adelaide – security and the suburbs never really appealed to him and when he was old enough to drive he blew out of town and headed bush. Twenty years and about two hundred jobs later, Phil's still out there roaming around going from job to job and place to place and meeting all sorts of characters along the way. Described by Westpac Bank as 'nomadic' – he is a financial disaster with no fixed address – But shit! ... whichever way you look at it he's got some great stories to tell! And in his own unique way Phil has turned drifting around outback Australia into an art form.

Disclaimer
This book is sold subject to the condition that it shall be taken in the spirit
it was intended – a light-hearted look at some of life's often tricky situations.
Some of the personal names included in this book have been changed or
only first names given, to protect the privacy of those concerned.

ISBN 0 646 39314 6

101 Adventures That Have Got Me Absolutely Nowhere

by

PHIL O'BRIEN

Cover, layout and typesetting by Geoff Morrison,
Bodgie Graphics, 16 Cove Street, Birchgrove, NSW 2041.

Photography by Sophie Howarth, PO Box 3031, Tamarama,
NSW 2026

Acknowledgments
Many thanks to Allan Hoffmann who really helped keep this
thing on the rails and a special thanks to my sister Marilyn
who slogged it out hour after hour on a crazy computer that
I'm sure had a mind of its own – and to her credit, she didn't
put her boot through the screen– as she so often threatened!
Sophie Howarth for generously supplying some great photos.
My old mate Geoff Morrison for doing such a terrific job with
the art work and typesetting, making a silk purse out of a
sow's ear.
A cold beer is in store for a writer and top bloke David Harris,
who's encouragement and direction was invaluable in seeing
this project through.

Mail Order enquiries to
Campfire Singer Productions, Box 257, Katherine, NT, Australia 0850.
Email: campfiresinger@hotmail.com

I'd like to dedicate this book to the open road,
a good steak sandwich ...

... and the people you meet along the way.

Holding a chook while sitting on a cactus in 1963 was probably the first real adventure that got me absolutely nowhere. (The author age 3 - Tempe Downs, Northern Territory)

Contents

THE GREYHOUND BUS DROPPED ME just outside the old bush pub, probably what you'd call the nerve centre of a bustling town of about fifteen people.

Although it wasn't the end of the world, you just had to shut your eyes and you could sense it wasn't real far away.

Thinking back...

I was a young bloke that was going to take the bush by storm, you know what I mean, I was gunna ride everything, break in everything, castrate everything, dehorn everything ... and make love to anything.

I was going places.

Adventure and romance... here we go. Let me at it!

I'd lined myself up a job on a cattle station, about 250 km from nowhere, and the manager, a bloke that went by the name of 'Old Morris', was due to fly in and pick me up in his aeroplane about midday, but I was a bit early, so I thought I'd give the local economy a boost and bang a few cold ones down while I waited.

As per usual, one lead to about six as I yarned to the barman and an old rabbit shooter that had wandered in. Looking back, I was glad I got the opportunity to have a few quick beers because I think it actually helped numb the senses a bit, although I didn't realise it, a terrifying ordeal was just around the corner... and I mean around the corner ... literally!

Sure enough, I could hear the drone of an aircraft coming in, louder and louder, until it sounded like the plane had landed and taxied in right up to the back door of the pub and I'll be buggered – It had!

I grabbed me swag and headed out ... and there he was...

'Old Morris'.

He was standing in front of the plane completely motionless, like some kind of stone monument. His forearms were huge and they hung down around his waist as if he was about to draw a gun. His hat was a real ball tearer and with the sun behind it, it cast a huge shadow out across the red dirt as if he was standing under some kind of rock overhang.

He must have been about 70, I guessed. He just stared at me. He was built like a Besser Block Shithouse, still powerful for his age, sun dried and tough. Without a doubt the bloke was 100% country and he didn't come across as a real chatty sort of guy.

He sized me up not looking real impressed, and I'm thinkin', this bloke could easy be mistaken for a rock carving – he was motionless.

Then out of the blue, he raised his arm and jerked his thumb back in the direction of the aircraft and I figured, this is it ...it was time to fly.

Now the plane looked like an old Toyota Corolla with wings, and when we climbed in, 'Old Morris's' hat took up two thirds of the cabin space, not leaving me much room at all. He still hadn't spoken.

So about now I was startin' to feel a little nervous, as I hate flying at the best of times, and Morris's rig wasn't a real late model job. It looked more like something he put together himself out in the back shed over a couple of Sundays.

He started clawing at the dash, then pulled something, then twisted something and then really reefed on something and the old girl fired. He gave it some herbs and we chugged off down the gravel strip, waves of red dust going everywhere.

I was feeling extremely anxious about the whole turnout and thoughts of Buddy Holly's air disaster came drifting through my mind. Then 'Old Morris' must have figured it was time to give her full throttle, because he nearly tore it clean out the dash!

After a wild buck we pig-rooted off across the flat, Morris at the helm with a look on his face that said 'he was gunna take this baby to hell and back', and I was strappin' in hoping the hell he makes it! So somehow we defied gravity and 'Old Morris' had her going straight up, I mean it wasn't a gradual ascent, we were just blasting straight up. Morris leaning back in the seat with his legs stretched out in front of him, as if he was in the saddle, completely expressionless.

Now to say at this stage I was getting a wee bit concerned doesn't really cover it, more like I was shitting heat beads for the webber BBQ might be slightly more accurate. Me and Morris weren't exactly chewing the fat either, which made things more tense.

I looked out and noticed the rivets on the wing were rattling around loosely, this was no joke.

Then he completely let go of the controls, leant back, pulled out his tobacco and proceeded to roll himself a smoke.

Now the plane was going all over the place like one of those acrobatic planes at an air show doing loop the loops. I was fairly stressing, trying to think of an appropriate prayer that covers air disasters!

Finally Morris finished building the cigarette, and as he hung it off his bottom lip, he decided to grab the controls again and level out which was a good move as we seemed to be going that far up.

I'm sure we weren't far from launching straight out into outer space, now we couldn't have been far off, I'm thinkin', and every time I looked out the window, all I could see was the rivets rattling around on the wing and I'm sure there wasn't as many there as when we first started!

The smoke from Morris's rollie was now starting to engulf the cabin and it was getting hard to breath, I shut my eyes and half expected us to blow up any minute, going through the sky like a comet.

Next thing he starts clutching at his chest and through the smoke haze pulls a little transistor radio from his pocket, pokes it at me and says *"get a score."* 'Old Morris' was a man of few words... three to be exact.

So, I presumed he meant cricket score as I knew the 'Aussies' were playing the 'Kiwis' at that time, but no luck, it was all static.

So on we sailed and I'm starting to think when God made man, I'm sure he didn't intend for him to be this high off the ground, no way! And I'm sure there were less rivets on the wing than there was five minutes ago. Morris's flying machine's falling to pieces, I'm sure of it, I was working myself up into a state of sheer uncontrollable terror. I was ready to shit volcanic rock.

'Old Morris' going for the tobacco again as calm as you like, and here we go again ... no hands!

Onwards we soared, the plane shooting all over the sky, Morris trying to get his lighter to work and finally thank God, it did. Then out came the transistor again, 'Old Morris' clamping it to his ear, and it sounded like he made contact.

The cricket score was priority number one, followed closely by the roll your own, then a bit further down the list was steering the plane.

The trip probably only took about one hour, but it felt like forever, it felt like I'd never been anywhere else but inside this plane shitting myself. But the tin roofs of the station finally came into view and I nearly burst into tears from joy, and it was the first time since we kicked off that I felt we might actually make it alive.

So Morris sent her straight down like a dive bomber, there was no gradual descent, he was taking the direct approach.

Down we shot and I could feel the 'G-forces' contorting my face. 'Old Morris' relentless, transistor clamped on his ear, smoke billowing from his gob just kept her going straight for the shiny tin roofs.

Down we speared, me clawing at the armrest, feeling like I was just about to lose my lunch and the six cans of beer I slugged down before joining 'Old Morris's' flying circus.

Morris was still transfixed, he looked as if he was going into bomb Pearl Harbour.

The tin roofs getting nearer by the second, trees looming closer and closer, he was taking her down in true 'Kamikaze' fashion. A shed was coming up and I'm thinkin', is he gunna make it?

Aaaaaaaaah!   ... just.

There wouldn't have been more than a cigarette paper in it as we skimmed over the corrugated iron roof. Morris unfazed, banking hard left to avoid wearing a windmill, then on down to the airstrip and as the wheels touched down the red dust exploded and 'Old Morris', the transistor radio, myself and the rivets rattled on down the airstrip, rocks pinging everywhere as he taxied the old girl through a sea of bull dust up to the shed we'd nearly collected a few minutes ago.

Morris cut the engine and jerked a thumb in the direction of the door, so I climbed out and, fairly jelly legged, I ducked around the corner for an extremely well deserved leak.

When I came back I could see him walking off, tranny still fixed to one ear, he was heading for the homestead, casual as you like.

Without a doubt, this trip did nothing to build up my confidence in flying, but one thing for sure, hell, it felt great to still be alive!

During the next three months there were thrills and spills aplenty, mad horses and even madder cattle. It was a rough, tough old life out in the Stock Camp at that place. It opened my eyes as a young bloke and the aboriginal stockmen who worked there were inspirational. There was nothing they couldn't do, and most of the time with huge smiles splashed across their faces. They'd take on anything.

Old Morris made a few cameo appearances but I can't remember him actually speaking. He just used to make hand signals occasionally. He was a tough old bastard alright. His missus however had no trouble slappin' her jaws together. She slipped it into me a few times, and I felt her scorn over various issues. They were extremely straight laced and commanded a fair bit of discipline of the young blokes working there. It was always a test to try and measure up, but I reckoned I was holding my own, I'd been kicked, bitten and stomped on by just about every horse on the place but was quite prepared to stick it and make a go of it.

Then came Easter.

Little did I know, this outback bubble was just about to burst...

From the time 'Old Morris' had given me that hell ride in his 'flying tin can', till Easter, was roughly three months. Now ... the only women I saw in that period was Morris's old soup boner of a wife and one of his daughters. She looked like Morris with tits. Apparently he had another daughter who was not a bad bit of gear but I'll be buggered if I ever saw her. He must have had her pretty well hidden away. So female company was non existent.

As well as this incredible hardship, I had not had a beer the whole time. So to put it bluntly, me balls were hangin' that low they were starting to collect burrs, and the mere thought of a beer made me tongue swell, so when the word come down the line that we were goin' into town for the Easter race weekend, I was well and truly ready for a break.

When the day come to head off, I was chaffin. The next chain of events I can remember as clear as if it happened last week and I still get a laugh.

The head stockman and his family floated in a bit earlier in the day, and 'Old Morris' and his wife flew in, which left me and a few of the lads plus a couple of the aboriginal stockmen to make the trip in the old Toyota tray back.

It was about a 270 km trip on a not real good dirt track.

We jumped on the back, and with swags rolled, we rattled. The bloke driving was only 15 – didn't quite know what he was doing driving. I remember he was a bit of a suck-arse on occasions and the head stockman must have told him he could have a drive ... 'Bad move', I'm thinkin'. Then I seen his style, and then I starts thinkin' 'we're an accident waiting to happen' ... and sure enough skidding around a corner going too fast, we hit a big pot hole and one bloke fell out the back onto the road smashing up a few ribs and knockin' the hell out of himself.

We reversed up and put him back on the back. He was in a lot of pain so we decided to make a slight detour and head for this small aboriginal community as we knew there was a clinic there. We got him to the clinic and lucky the Sister was there on duty. She didn't seem real interested. The treatment he got left a lot to be desired – two panadol with some dencorub for the ribs.

But he seemed happy enough with that. I thought she could have done more. But that's just the way it was.

Meanwhile, outside at the Toyota, a crowd was forming. Everyone wanted a lift into town for the races, I'm startin' to think I'm never going to make it.

When we finally pulled out of the community, there would have been about 35 local people crammed on the back, not countin' dogs and babies on the breast. But fair enough no one wanted to miss out on the big weekend.

It was standing room only, believe me, as we headed on down the track. I was doin' it tough crammed in the back, and to make it worse, one bloke decided to try and have a leak while we were travellin'.

He had the right idea, tryin' to shoot it over the edge of the tray, but because of the speed we were going, it just came spraying back on everybody – mainly me. Yeah! I wore most of it and I was startin' to feel a bit jaded.

We finally made town about late afternoon sometime.

We dropped off the mob and poked on over to the show grounds, about half a kilometre from the pub. Now, all the station people were camped around there, and us young blokes were expected to help set 'Old Morris' and his missus up, get them fire wood and stuff like that, be good ambassadors for the station etc.

The head stockman was there and his family. They were also settin' up.

Now you didn't have to be a Philadelphia Lawyer to work out the piss wasn't gunna flow in this camp I'm thinkin'. It was gunna be billy tea and sandwiches with no one sowin' any wild oats. So I figured it was time to do a bit of foxin' and get me arse over to the pub.

I threw me swag out of the Tojo, grabbed my money I had stashed, and told everyone I was off to make a couple of phone calls.

I headed off down the track with three months pay burning in my pocket. I couldn't wait to smash into it.

On the way, I passed the showground. The mob there looked as if they were getting ready for a big night at the hall. There were balloons going up, women and kids poking around, and I think there was some kind of 'do' on there later, something to do with the race meeting. But the way I figured, it was probably a real family affair. Morris and the gang would probably be there. They were all so straight laced and expected the same of their workers, you know what I mean, don't tarnish the good name sort of caper ... but I wasn't buying in.

Call it a sixth sense or maybe divine intervention, but I just knew the place to be was the little pub and I couldn't have been more right.

The joint was rockin' all right. The first beer went down that well, it brought tears to me eyes and I nearly passed out. It was a great atmosphere, everyone yarning, mostly stockmen from various stations catching up. A few girls, not many, but then again I only wanted one, I'm thinkin' to myself.

It wasn't long before I was mixing in and chatting with blokes. The old rabbit shooter I met before was partaking, so I had a beer with him. He'd been doin' it hard, but was making a bit of beer money. I forgot about everything. I was just enjoying the cold beer. The hours just flew by.

The juke box was getting a fair shake up with Slim Dusty singing his guts out and the same Charlie Pride song seemed to be getting selected over and over. Everyone singing along and taking on freight like there was no tomorrow.

Now, I'm havin' the time of my life. It was getting on towards midnight and I had progressed onto rum and gone into second gear feeling pretty good. A couple of blokes had already choked out, slumped here, slumped there, the old rabbiter looked about set to 'Astral travel' any minute, but all in all, spirits were still high.

So, I have a bit of a look around the bar, seein' who's up who and who hadn't paid. I thought I noticed one girl checking me out. So I take another quick look around and sure enough, she's smiling at me. So, I returned the smile and tried to be a bit cool. Every time I looked over, she pretty well was looking my way, but she seemed to be with a bloke.

'Wouldn't that shit you' I'm thinkin', 'last girl left in the bar and she thinks I'm alright, but she's got a friggin' boyfriend hangin' off her.' Oh well, that's how it goes.

So, I hopped into my rum for a while and did a bit more singing and carrying on with the blokes I'd met... well all's not lost I thought, it had been a great night anyway.

A bit later, just out of curiosity, I looked around to see what she was up to, and to my surprise, her boyfriend had passed out drunk, and was curled up at her feet choked down like an old dog, totally out of it... very interesting I'm thinking.

Now I can remember this clear as day. I ordered another rum, took another squiz, and the girl's smiling right at me, then looking down at him, then smiling back at me. She did this a couple of times, like she was trying to tell me something.

Now me blood pressure's going up. It's going right up. Now I'm thinking if me blood pressure goes up any more, me head's gonna shoot clean off. I couldn't really work out why she zeroed in on me, I'm no oil painting, hadn't had a wash for a few days, I was caked in dust from the ride in, and smelled like stale piss!

She actually wasn't bad looking herself, especially for this time of night. She was making eyes now. This was getting serious. Waves of passion, like an electric current, were washing up and down my body. 'This was real Mills and Boon' I'm thinkin'. Then, fairly casually, she up and walked out in the direction of the outside dunny. A faint heart never won a fair maiden, I said to myself, as I decided to head out to the loo as well, hoping to run into her and maybe start a bit of a yak or something.

I had no idea what was about to take place.

She came out of nowhere, lunging at me with her tongue stuck out in front of her like an old goanna. She grabbed me and jammed if fair down me throat and we went into a clinch.

After every bit of oxygen had been drained out of me, we finally unplugged for a breath, then hooked straight back up like a set of uni-joints. There was no time for conversation, things were just too intense.

We were somewhere in the shadows between the pub and the outside dunny lovin' up big time and things were happening pretty quick.

We'd already crossed the line over from passion, and we were starting to head in the direction of reckless abandon, so I put the brakes on for a minute and suggested we walk back to the camp ground where me swag was located and maybe 'chew the fat' there for a while.

She was all for it.

Now, she was a pretty girl, well dressed, well spoken, and I'm thinkin', 'maybe she's not getting enough attention from her boyfriend, maybe we'd met in a past life, maybe it was that stale piss smell that sent her. Who knows?'

She was keen alright, but at that stage, there was no time to analyse the situation, it didn't matter. I was half cut with three months worth of oats saved up and it looked like I might be doin' some sowin'.

As we walked, we talked a bit. She was a governess just come in for the race meeting. So, on we strolled like old lovers do ... you know ... whispering, cooing, purring, kissing, holding, Mills and Booning until somewhere between the show ground and the camp-ground, it all got too much, I mean, we started to get it on then and there.

I was gonna take her to places she'd never been before right on the side of the road, and she was enjoying the trip.

Now, there wasn't really a problem with that, not really any problem at all. We were both consenting young people, ships in the night, victims of love, whichever way you look at it. Having a knee trembler on the side of a quiet dirt track under the glorious territory sky seemed like the right thing to do at the time, absolutely no problem.

Unfortunately, the 'do' at the showgrounds had come to an end, pretty well about the same time we decided to kick off...

All the people from that turn out, women and kids, 'Old Morris' etcetera, etcetera, were getting in their vehicles getting ready to poke off down the track back to the camp ground. They had no idea Romeo and Juliet would be goin' nineteen to the dozen on the side of the road in full view.

Sure enough, up the road they came, like a procession, all doin' about 20 mile an hour. There must have been twenty or thirty vehicles heading back to the camp ground. By the time the procession got to us, we were goin' at it like a couple of camp dogs. Her dress was up around her head and she was bent forward a bit, and behind her, was me with me trousers concertinered down around me ankles and I was goin' hammer and tong.

'Oh shit' I'm thinkin, 'friggin hell', I hadn't counted on this.

I'm thinking what's a bloke meant to do. But, it was too late ... they were on us, high beam flashing, horns beeping, wolf whistles, screams, kids yelling, the full bloody bit!

We just kept on going.

I decided, 'bugger it', I wasn't stopping for anyone.

She was alright, because she had her head covered by her dress – she was kind of incognito.

I glanced down at one vehicle and a woman was trying to cover her kids eyes. Next thing I knew, 'Old Morris' goes cruisin' past sitting in the passenger seat of some Toyota, smoke hangin' off his bottom lip, staring straight at me.

He looked totally dumb founded as he took a double take.

'You wouldn't read about it' I'm thinkin'. 'You wouldn't effin read about it ... ', figured his missus would have been in there too somewhere, no doubt she would have been jaw slappin' all the way back to the campground. The look on 'Old Morris's' face was one of total disbelief like he'd just seen a ghost.

The cars had all finally gone past. Of course, it seemed like a long time, but the whole episode probably wasn't more than a few minutes.

'Darkness again, thank God', I said, standing there jelly legged, strides still down.

Thinking back, I knew I was in the shit with Morris and them. I mean, I would have had to have been, taking off, getting pissed and then the big how you goin' on the side of the road. I mean it didn't look real good. I was representing the station alright but not quite in the manner 'Old Morris' had intended. But anyway, off we went still headin' for me swag. We were getting all set for Act II. I still had a bit of lead in me pencil and she was pretty well in for what ever was going.

So off we wandered. We found me swag and were into it again ... with gusto.

Somewhere down the line I must have passed out and she floated, because in the morning, I woke up, bright day light, completely naked, laying on my back on my swag.

I sat up. To my horror, a crowd had formed.

There's 'Old Morris', his missus, the head stockman, his family and quite a mob of other people staring straight at me, pointing and carrying on.

Their jaws seemed to be working overtime. Even Morris's secmed to be going up and down. Yep, that was the clincher alright. Bloody fan, bloody tastic, I thought, feeling like shit, a real spectacle, everyone staring and such, as if they were waiting for the Second Coming, and I was the support act.

So with me head hung low, I got dressed, rolled me swag and took off. And no point lookin' back either because the jury looked as if it had come to a decision, and probably not a real favourable one either.

Without a doubt this adventure was well and truly over!

> Remember... when you go into town on a BENDER, DON'T camp near the Boss!

Penthouse Players

ONE THING FOR SURE, NO MATTER WHO YOU ARE or where you come from, there is always that one time in your life when you can honestly say 'you were down on your luck' and things just didn't pan out the way you'd planned and the old bank account is looking a little like Lake Eyre – empty!

Now a bush job I had, had fallen through and I found myself down in Perth, no money, no job, no friends, no nothing, just an old Holden ute and a little bit of change I'd found under the seat.

I was cuttin' it fine.

The big decision that I had to make, was whether to spend the cash on a few beers or buy a couple of tins of baked beans to avoid starving to death. But then ... there really wasn't much of a decision at all. I simply took the most mature and obvious option and marched straight into the Cottlesloe Hotel.

Now this was actually a stroke of good luck, 'cause while I was in there hangin' off a middy, I got yarnin' to this bloke and I told him my situation.

Well, it just so happened he knew a bit of work that was going. He reckoned it was a bit different but the money is OK ... I was all ears.

"This one mob's lookin' for drivers", he reckoned.

I said "driving what, taxis, trucks or what?"

"It's with this mob called Penthouse Players, it's an escort agency" he reckoned. "You cart this prostitute around and while she is inside Hawkin the Fork, you wait outside and make sure everything is OK and when the time is up, you drive her to the next job, it's as easy as that – I'm doing a bit of driving for them myself, hardly any trouble, easy money."

'Shit!' I'm thinkin, 'this isn't my usual line of work, but what the hell, I needed to make a few bucks to get out of the scrape I was in'. "Yeah ..., I'll give it a go." So he gave me the address and I went straight around there.

Now after a slight altercation with a german shepherd, I finally made it to the front door and rang the bell. A middle aged lady answered. I told her my story. She sized me up very carefully and then took me into her office. There was about thirty phones on this one desk and they were ringing like crazy. Every time she picked one up, she would answer with a different name. Like – "Hi, this is Penthouse Players" or "gidday this is Golden Girls", or "welcome, this is Luscious Ladies."

Obviously, most of these different escort agencies around town were really the one place.

The old girl just farms the jobs out to all these ladies she's got working for her, rings them up and gives them the addresses of the clients and off they go out there. Thanks for coming ... literally.

She asked me a lot of questions then told me she had a new girl that needed a driver. Maggie, a pommy girl, she reckoned. In Australia on a working holiday.

The old duck told me "in this game, no one uses their real name, so what will we call you?" I said, "just call me Tom" - she said,"we've already got a Tom", so I suggested Major Tom after a song I heard on the radio. So from then on, as far as she was concerned, I was Major Tom.

So off I go to pick up Maggie.

Now one of these days, I'm gonna get a normal job like everyone else, I swear it.

Maggie's door was wide open, so I gave a "hoi" and I heard a faint "just come in", so I walked in and all of a sudden the bathroom door opens and out walks Maggie in all her naked glory, as casual as you like. She must have had a bit of greek in her or something, because she had an incredible amount of body hair and I'm thinkin, 'if she ever did her bikini line, there'd be enough just in the off cuts alone, to knit a polar neck jumper.'

Which ever way you looked at it, she was well thatched.

"You must be Major Tom, have a seat and I'll just get ready" she reckoned. When she came out all dressed up, she reminded me of a fancy dress I went to once when this truckie friend of mine came dressed as a woman. Just like him, she moved really awkwardly in these incredible high heels.

I liked her, she was straight up and very friendly and we hit it off really well. She was just tryin' to make a buck. Nothing more nothing less.

We sat around talking for a while, then HQ rang and said they had a heap of work lined up, so off we sailed in the HR ute from one client to the next. I'd just ring Headquarters and they'd give me the addresses and old Maggie would produce the goods and I'd just wait out in the ute. When the time was up, if she didn't come straight out, I'd just go and knock on the door and she'd come out and off we'd go again, no problems. All over Perth we went.

She'd see about eight to ten clients a night and I'd get $15 a pop, which in those days was pretty good. Roughly, I was pulling $100 per night plus the lovely Maggie would fill up the ute as well.

I never tried for a freebie, because after a long night, you wouldn't know whose porridge you'd be stirring, and it put me off a bit.

But, although she was a little plain, and a little hairy, she had a lovely personality and after a couple of weeks, we'd really turned into a good team. As far as any trouble went, we had a really good run and I was starting to relax a bit. Then came the weekend, the American Navy came to town, about 3 destroyers worth. The phones at Head quarters were ringing hot. Every sailor must have had a sack full, because old Maggie was flat out.

Somewhere around 4 in the morning, Maggie felt totally shagged out and was ready to call it a night, so I rang HQ and they pleaded. "Can you see the one more", so the good scout she was, Maggie agreed.

It was another sailor staying at this motel in Fremantle. So, off we went.

It was a one-hour booking and I was sitting out in the ute playing a Slim Dusty cassette, trying to stay awake. Finally the hour was up, but no Maggie. So I went to the motel room and knocked on the door half-asleep, not expecting any trouble ... all of a sudden I hear Maggie screaming inside the room *"let me go, let me go."*

Amidst a lot of crashing and banging, there was this other voice, a really deep, strong, gravelly voice with a strong American accent. I'm thinking there's either a bad rap song playing in there or Maggie's in the shit...

So I went for the door, and to my relief it wasn't locked. As I opened it, there was this huge naked Negro running amuck.

Maggie was cowering in the corner. This Negro looked big, black and bad and reminded me of one of those giant basketballers.

He swung around and come at me and I couldn't help but notice his 'old fella', I'm thinkin', 'the last time I seen a pizzle like that, it was hangin' off a Brahman bull.' It come complete with a huge set of black haggots to match. They drooped down like 2 big black bags of marbles.

Maggie wasn't wastin' any time, she grabbed her gear and flew past me going out the door doing 90.

So he flies at me ... there was no time to think, just enough time to do what any respectable citizen would have done in my position – kick him fair in the cods – I mean, you couldn't miss!

And then it was exit stage right.

I took off down the corridor of this motel stridin' right out. I caught Maggie on the first bend and then accelerated past her. She was movin' fast, but no match for Major Tom. By the time I got to the ute, my RM Williams riding boots were smokin ... I'd laid rubber on every bend. By the time Maggie made the ute, I had it idling ready to go, and we didn't look back.

I give it away after that. I'd stashed a bit of money and I figured I'd quit while I was ahead.

As far as I know, Maggie continued on her working holiday.

And as for the big Negro prick, well, I hope he ended up with a very painful throbbing set of 'emu eggs'!

THE DUPONTS WERE A COUPLE of your regular every day multi millionaires from Paris, and all they ever wanted was a nice quiet holiday in Australia – you know – nothing more, nothing less.

They were sick of the 'Riviera', and the South of Spain was getting so crowded, and Club Med Monaco, well ... that would always be there next year – so why not sip a few cocktails at some exclusive resort in sunny Australia, they reckoned.

Nothing too strenuous, maybe venture out of the air con in the late afternoon and hold a koala or, if they were feeling adventurous, maybe have a real outdoors experience – you know, a game of golf or something.

Roughing it to the Duponts was having to line up at the bank. Well fair enough, different strokes for different folks, no worries at all.

Everything would have been alright except for the fact, someone sold them the wrong trip. Some travel agent stuffed up big time. It must have been when they got to Australia because their English was pretty bad so I'd say that's where their misunderstanding took place. Instead of them going to some ritzy country club they ended up getting sent to a remote Kimberley cattle station where I was working.

And this place was Bloody Rough as Guts too, I mean I didn't even know what I was doing there...

I couldn't believe it when the Boss of the station calls up and says "There's two French millionaires on the way. Go and meet them at the river." Of course the Boss wasn't living there, he had more brains than that, the joint was even too rough for him. There wasn't much cattle work either – all the cattle had run off, the place was even too rough for them as well.

There were just a few silly bastards living there like me that had nowhere else to go in the middle of the wet season.

Rivers were flooding, it was stinking hot, humidity was up to 193% and there was a snake on every corner, not to mention the rats, and scorpions and stuff. 'Why the hell would two millionaires from Paris want to experience this?', I'm thinkin'. I was pullin' out myself as soon as the rivers went down. I was sick of dodgin' snakes, sick of dodgin' crocs and sick of dodgin' rats.

So the Boss rings back to make sure we got the message – right: two French tourists: pick up: river: sunset. Yeah, got that, yeah got that. And yeah we will look after them.

What the hell's goin' on, we're wonderin'. I knew they'd planned to try and get a few tourists up here in the dry season, but that was a long way off. And not your everyday tourists either, probably 4-wheel drive enthusiasts or fishermen, you know Adventure Tourism, Gung Ho stuff. It was just too far between cocktails for the Upmarket mob. Anyway mine was not to reason why, mine was just to pick 'em up at the River.

So I hooked up the little boat trailer and headed off through the hills slowly winding down to the river. The river, just quietly, was a bloody raging, roaring torrent about half a kilometre wide. The Boss had apparently hired someone to drive them out from Kununurra Airport after they flew in from Sydney. Then it was about a three hour drive to the river. I was to go across the river in the tinny and pick 'em up then ferry them back across, then up to the station for their relaxing holiday in Paradise.

One look at the river and I'm thinkin', 'I hope they're good swimmers if something goes wrong because it was fairly rippin' down.'

Still at this late stage the Duponts would have thought they were heading for an exclusive Country Club and the vehicle that was to pick them up at the airport was an air-conditioned 4-wheel drive so I doubt the penny would've dropped.

I'd say when they got to the rip roaring, half a kilometre wide, screaming, surging river three hours later – with no sign of a Country Club in sight, not even a little one, I'd say at a rough guess it would probably have hit 'em about then. You know they possibly would have got an inkling something was amiss.

When I got to the river I could see them on the other side, two figures dressed completely in white. In the distance they looked like two boundary umpires. I'm thinkin' pretty ambitious wearing white in this country as I launched the 10-ft dinghy into the water. I was feelin' a little toey myself, there were logs and branches and all sorts of stuff eddying around, not to mention the odd floating handbag or two. ' A bloke could come unstuck here very easy', I'm thinkin'.

The water was rushing too fast for me to go directly across so I had to head downstream and then edge me way across bit by bit and then come up the other side into the current. The two figures in white on the other side didn't seem to be moving much, they looked very still and rigid, they were just staring at the river.

It probably took me a good 15 minutes to get across there and as I came closer I couldn't help but take a double take at the Duponts. They were in absolute pristine condition, everything about them was bloody immaculate. I'd never seen anyone so well presented. They must have been pedicured, manicured, facialled, waxed,

polished, nipped, tucked and lippo-sucked. They were fuckin'
Designer! ...and totally colour co-ordinated.

They looked as if they should have been a display in some store's
front window. Both in brilliant white outfits with matching slip-ons,
they were absolutely spectacular.

I pulled in and yelled; *"Gooday... Gooday. How goes it?"* But no reply.
The Duponts were in shock. They just stared through me at the
river. Then the bloke that dropped them off gave me a wink and
said, "I'll see you back here in a week." He took off and I could see
he was pissing himself laughing as he pulled out.

The Duponts' faces had gone the same colour as their designer
colour coordinated outfits - White. They were terrified.

The Old Boy couldn't speak any English at all and she could only
speak a real little bit. They started mumbling and carrying on but
it was hard to hear them above the roar of the river. I tried to
explain we had to go - "it's getting dark, very dangerous – very dangerous", I'm sayin'. But I think they'd worked that one out by
themselves. So I gestured to Mrs Dupont to get in the dinghy and it
was like I'd asked her to Walk the Plank or something...

I finally got her in, then the Old Boy – but getting him in was like
trying to coax a cat down from the tree. But we finally were all in
and I pushed off. You know the worst thing that can happen in a
small dinghy, is if someone moves suddenly to one side, the boat can
tip over before you know it. Well, I didn't have to worry with the
Duponts, they just wedged themselves in and they never moved an
inch. Their knuckles were glowing white from gripping the side of
the tinny.

They were petrified.

On the other side I had to carry Mrs Dupont from the boat to the
dry land as she didn't want to get her designer footwear wet, 'well
fair enough', I'm thinkin, but then the Old Boy pulls the same stunt
and I had to carry him as well. I thought that was a bit rough, but

fair enough they were on holidays I suppose. Anyway it was probably just an old French tradition.

We tried to communicate a bit on the way back to the station. They seemed pretty concerned as to where I was taking them. I tried to keep them relaxed but they were shitting themselves. I mean they were really wound up. It was like we were heading to a work camp in Siberia, or something.

They just didn't seem to be in a festive holiday mood at all.

Back at the station I showed them their room. They couldn't believe it. I think they thought they'd died and gone to Bonanza. Admittedly the rooms were rough – old sheets of rusty corrugated iron and stone floor. The stone floors were pretty wild, not much effort had gone into making them level. Walking into one of those rooms was like walking up a creek bed.

The Duponts' first night of their holiday could have probably gone smoother but we tried our best. As it was an extremely hot and sticky night we put the Duponts in a room where the corrugated iron wall didn't quite meet the corrugated iron roof, a gap of about a metre was between the two. I thought the room might be a bit breezier for them plus it had a good ceiling fan.

This was all great in theory till in the middle of the night a fruit bat flies in and gets chopped to pieces by the ceiling fan, followed later on by another one. Actually this was quite common at that place. I think all that corrugated iron upset the inbuilt radar of the bats somehow. But you try telling that to two distraught French millionaires: all they could say was: "*le blood, le blood, le chomp, le chomp.*"

I really felt sorry for them, they must have been up all night by the look and anyway they wanted out. They didn't care how – but they wanted out!

I explained the airstrip at the station was under water and the only way out was the way they came in – across the river, and the bloke from Kununurra won't be back for a week. So they moped around like they were next in line for the Electric Chair, draggin' the designer slip-ons through the dirt ... they looked down and out you know ... like the stock market had just crashed.

The next drama was the outdoor shower. Mr Dupont's scrubbin' up and a giant green tree frog jumps onto his back. He nearly screamed the place down. Then the old girl goes to use the dunny and she starts screamin': apparently one of the dogs had dragged a snake in there and must have been chewin' on it in the shade of the shithouse.

See for us, all this stuff was normal. But the Duponts were takin' it pretty rough.

It was one thing after the other. And by late that day every one was ready for a drink, including me. So we sat around in the cool of the afternoon and gave the Duponts a couple of stiff ones. We'd soon all worked out there had been a big mistake with their holiday arrangements. We sympathized and they really didn't seem like bad folks. We yarned as best we could considering the language problem and things were settling down nicely, a couple more drinks, a few laughs, you could almost say they started to relax – not quite – but almost.

Then a beautiful little crimson finch turns up, you know a really pretty little bird and the Duponts are really excited by this exquisite little finch. So they're checkin' it out and I'm thinkin', 'they're startin' to loosen up, good on you finch', I'm thinkin'.

Then out of nowhere drops a python and within a split second is squeezing the shit out of the bird. I couldn't believe it. The Duponts were hysterical. And now the snake's tryin' to swallow it, so one bloke gets the shot gun and unloads on the snake, *KABOOM*, he misses and shoots a hole in the wall, the snake drops the bird and it falls down on the ground at the feet of the Duponts. The Duponts freak, one of the dogs runs in and swallows the finch and runs off leaving the snake wriggling around at the feet of the Duponts. Mr Dupont's doin' a tap dance and the Old Girl's tryin' to get on a table.

I mean it was a pantomime. I finally pissed the snake off with a stick but that was it, the poor buggers were really rattled after that one. Old boy reckons "*le snake, le boom, le chomp ... le mad house.!*"

So we sat them down and pumped a few more drinks into them. Mrs Dupont was that wound up she looked down at the designer logo on the pocket of her top and went crazy, brushing at it with her hand, screaming – she thought it was something crawling up her shirt. Her nerves must have been shot. Eventually she realized it was just a logo and calmed down a bit.

"*I cannot live with ze animals*", she reckons. 'Oh well ... only another six days to go', I'm thinkin'.

That night the Boss rings up and wants to know how it's goin'. I told him it wasn't. He made out to be a bit surprised but I think he was making a few bucks out of it somehow, I doubt the Duponts were getting this fabulous holiday for free, that was for sure. Reluctantly he agreed to try and get the guy out from Kununurra a few days early. He was gunna be in touch.

Well anyway the Duponts got through another night, this time they didn't use the ceiling fan, they figured it was better to sweat it out than get showered with bat guts again.

Apart from two bush rats mating under the bed, it was a pretty quiet night.

The next day someone came up with an idea to take them on an outing to this local waterfall. Maybe have a BBQ and boil the billy, give them a paddle in one of the rock pools, you know – get 'em out there doin' a bit.

It was a particularly stinkin' hot day but it looked like the rain might hold off at least, so we loaded them into this 4 wheel drive with some meat and stuff for the day, and this one bloke who knew the area pretty well volunteered to take them. They seemed happy enough when they left. 'Maybe this could be the turning point', I'm thinkin', 'maybe this could just be the day they decide the outback isn't such a bad place after all.' Yep, could be a definite conversion coming up here, they'll probably come back bright eyed and bushy tailed just on sunset and tell me all about it – Happy as Larry. '*Le great*', they'll probably reckon'.

So feelin' good, I set about catching up on a few jobs around the place now that the Duponts were out of my hair. I poked around then decided I'd do a rubbish run in the old tractor, so I grabbed as much rubbish as I could find and loaded it in the bucket of the tractor.

It was stifling hot so I thought I'd have a cup of tea and a sit down in the shade for a minute before driving off to the dump.

I suppose it had been a good two hours since the Duponts had left for the big day out. No doubt they were out there somewhere having fun, I'm thinkin'. So I pokes off in the old tractor headin' for the dump, bouncin' along the road, sun beatin' down.

I turn a corner and there staggerin' down the track is the Fucking Duponts. What the...?

Their white designer coordinated outfits were caked with sweat and mud and they were stuffed. I mean they were really rooted, barely getting one foot in front of the other. I reckon' another hour in the sun and they would have been dead. Anyway Mrs Dupont staggers up to the tractor, her face like a tomato and her lips like two dried apricots and she reckons "le bog, le bog, le bog" and then the old boy starts up "le bog" and wavin' his arms around.

Apparently they'd driven about 10 kilometres down the road and the bloke driving pulled off the road to show them an old set of cattle yards and they got bogged up to the doors in mud. The driver was still back there diggin' it out. The Duponts thought they could walk back as there was bugger all shade out there. They thought they could handle the walk.

Well 10 kilometres goes forever when you're not used to the heat as they found out. So they flopped in the bucket with all the rubbish and I headed home.

'If only the Paris mob could see them now', I'm thinkin', 'choked down in the bucket amongst the garbage, bouncin' down the road in the old station tractor'. They were a real mess covered in mud and shit and on their last legs. Absolutely exhausted, you could hardly even tell they were wearing carefully colour coordinated designer outfits either.

Back at the station the Duponts laid pretty low, the gas had been knocked out of them, the poor buggers. I sort of felt sorry for them; all they ever wanted was a quiet holiday.

I was bloody thankful the Boss came good and organised that bloke to be at the river a few days early because it really wasn't coming together for the Duponts. And when I told them we could get them out early, their faces lit up, just like Robinson Crusoe's must have when he'd seen that ship on the horizon.

The Duponts nearly broke down and wept.

So later on we forged the mighty river again. The Duponts hangin' on that tight when we got to the other side they had aluminium wedged under their finger nails.

Once again I had to lift Mrs Dupont out onto the dry ground and same with the old Boy, I don't blame him. His designer slip-ons probably cost him more than I was makin' in a month up at 'The Last Frontier Holiday Centre for Wayward French Millionaires'.

So we said our good-byes and they pleaded with me to come with them, get away from this place they reckon'.

Well they meant well ... but I told them I wouldn't be far behind them, once the river goes down anyway. And as they took off I'm thinkin' 'Yeah, you got it mate, the sooner I get out of this place the better – and that's for *Le Bloody Sure*!'

I ALWAYS ENJOYED DOIN' A BIT OF STATION WORK. It never pays much but, shit, you'd have some wild times ... and in this day and age of technology as it is, it's great to still be able to do a day's work on the back of a horse. It's an honest and uncomplicated life – that's providing you can stay on the back of the horse you're meant to be riding...

Alladin was the Dirtiest ... Sneakiest ... Rottenest ... Charf-guzzlin' ... Brumby Bastard of a horse I ever come across. He was a total prick and I'd like to really emphasize that. I crossed paths with him up on a cattle place in northern Western Australia, and me and that horse fought World War III all by ourselves.

At that time the station was gearing up for the first muster of that year. Now this can be a pretty exciting time on most properties as all the working horses usually hadn't been ridden since the last muster the previous year, maybe 4-5 months or so. They come in fresh and generally with a bit of attitude.

Alladin came in fresh alright, and he came in with plenty of attitude, and believe me it was all bad.

He was a big strong good looking horse. He looked like he had a bit of breeding in him and I think this is what saved him, otherwise I'd say someone would have shot him years ago. I have to say when I first seen him in the paddock I noticed his good looks. He moved really well. I thought maybe a bit long in the leg but he sure looked like he could really go.

Of course I was new on the place and I didn't know the history of the horse. I never had any idea of the pain and suffering he'd instilled in the hearts of many a bloke before me. It dawned on me something was amiss the day the head stockman was allocating horses.

I ended up with Alladin.

Now all the other blokes cracked up laughing and I'm thinkin' 'Hang on here'. Then this old aboriginal bloke makes the Sign of the Cross and they all crack up again! It was about then one thought entered my mind and one thought only and it flashed like a neon sign before me ... 'mongrel horse ... mongrel horse ...and you're stuck with it!'

Every station had a few, and it was usually the new bloke that got lumbered with them. The older blokes were usually too cunning.

I could see from the onset I was really going to earn my money on this place.

We brought all the horses in and yarded them at the homestead yards. The idea with horses that have been spelled for a while is to get them in and ride them and handle them for a bit, get them used to the idea it's working time again. Knock the gas out of them a bit.

So just like people have their little differences horses are no different, some go along with you and are quiet, you can jump straight on them no worries. Others will do anything to keep you and the saddle off their back, and then there's ones like Alladin that just plain have murder on their mind.

The other blokes started catching their particular horses and trying to get saddles on and stuff, it was the usual sideshow, people swearing, horses bolting around everywhere, dust, dust and more dust. Well this sort of atmosphere can unsettle a horse even more than what it already is, so I cut Alladin out of the mob and hunted him into a small holding yard by himself. He was flighty alright, kicking out with his legs, like some kind of martial art's expert, nostrils flaring, tail stuck up in the air, prancing around the yard, wild as shit.

I let him go for a minute hoping he'd puff himself out a bit, well anyway that was the theory. I let him go, and round and round he went. Then it was time to suck it and see. So I grabbed my bridle and cornered him and to my surprise and relief he was really easy to catch and I had no trouble slipping the bridle on him. But little did I know it was only the calm before the storm. Next step was the saddle blanket. As I went to slip it on he turned and bit me fair in the back, then spun around and cow kicked me in the shoulder. And I went down like a ton of bricks.

That was it, the co-operation between man and beast was over.

I was pulling myself out of the dirt when the head stockman came over, he'd obviously just recovered from a heavy bout of laughing – probably near pissed himself.

Alladin prancing around victorious, reigns dragging in the sand. Together me and the head stockman managed to catch him and get the saddle on its back. It was no mean feat with Alladin striking out with his front hoofs, lefts and rights reminiscent of the great Jeff Fenech in his prime.

This was it. Time to show him who's boss. I recited the 'Our Father', then sprung on.

Alladin went berserk – he raked, he twisted, he bucked and he rooted. This horse really had a red hot coal up his arse and he was tryin' to send me to the moon. I stuck with him for as long as my limited ability let me, but he ended up spearing me straight back into the dirt.

So flat on my back I'm layin' in the dust only half conscious hoping this is only a bad dream, and I should be waking up soon ... I opened my eyes and through the dust there's Alladin standing over me looking down. This was no dream. It was shaping up as more of a nightmare... and I'm thinkin' 'how do you get out of it?'

The head stockman helped me up onto my feet. He was weak from laughing so much, great, I thought, if I break me neck in this yard at least everyone's had a good laugh, yeah, at least it's been worthwhile.

Back onto Alladin I sprung. This time I was really pissed off, and I stuck to him like shit to a blanket. He couldn't budge me. He twisted and spun and hopped all over the place but I was still on. So old Alladin had to dig a bit deeper into his repertoire of tricks, and so the big prick rubbed me up along the rails of the yard 'til he finally scraped me off sending me down into the dirt once again. The dust cleared and there he was looking straight down at me – the horse from hell.

The head stockman came up grinning away, *"You got him beat, old mate, you got him beat"* he reckoned. I said "Thanks, that's great ... but can you go tell the horse that?"

I think I cracked a rib when he jammed me up against the rails, but pain or no pain this horse wasn't gunna beat me.

I decided to hobble his front legs, with a hobble strap to restrict his movements a bit, this was an old trick but 'all's fair in love and war and horses', I'm thinkin'. So on I go again. This time I had him, he performed but the hobbles slowed him up a bit. Around the yard we went and it seemed Alladin was settling down.

Normally the next step with a horse like this, once you've taken the edge off it a bit, is to take it out the yard for a bit of a run out on the flat... a bit of a canter, turning him this way, then that ... you know, a bit of discipline.

Well the hobbles came off and the gate was opened.

Alladin didn't just trot out, you couldn't even say he galloped out, it was like he was fired out of a cannon. He fucking rocketed out, the dirty stinking rotten hay-burning bastard he was, screamed out across the flat going as fast as any horse has ever gone in the history of mankind – and I couldn't pull him up. I tried everything. So much for the discipline. This horse was just a rebel without a cause.

So old Alladin still had a few tricks up his hoof, this was probably one of his favourites, the one where he kills the rider. So I stuck to him like glue, to come off at the speed he was going meant at least one or two broken bones, and that's one or two I didn't feel like breaking at the time.

This horse was doin' exactly what he wanted, I just happened to be on his back at the time!
Then Alladin played his trump, he hit the skids, the bastard had gone from about 227 mph to nothing... he propped and I just wasn't ready for it! I launched out of the saddle like I'd been catapulted – through the air I sailed then ...*KATHOONKAR*... touch down, me rib cage rattled like a set of wind chimes. The fall knocked every bit of wind out of me and after the dust settled I opened my eyes and there he was, the bay brumby bastard just peering down at me, and in between gags for breath, one thought entered my head – 'he wasn't gunna beat me, he wasn't gunna beat me!'

I got myself up on one knee still trying to get me lungs to pump a bit. I was feeling pretty buggered, couldn't believe he'd done what he'd done. Old Alladin could have took off if he pleased, but he must have preferred to hang around and just wallow in the euphoria of the moment. Anyway why would he take off now? He hadn't killed me yet. He'd come close with that last manoeuvre but no way was this spinifex chewin' poofta gunna beat me.

I got on my feet feeling like a half sucked Rice Bubble, 'gotta get through the pain barrier and beat this prick', I'm thinkin'. Pride was at stake now, it was do or die. I dragged myself up into the saddle, kicked him fair in the guts and off we went again. I'd told myself I'd be ready for him next time, gunna out think him, after all I had brains on my side – I was a human being, he was just a brumby prick!

So across the flat we flew, Alladin running on pure adrenaline and loving every minute of it, me clamped to the saddle, I wasn't gunna let him beat me! I was tensing up ready, I knew he'd try that trick again any minute now, any minute he's gunna prop, I was just waitin', no way was I leavin' the saddle this time, no way would this horse beat me.

Flat out we ripped across the open plain, then crunch, he hit the skids, but I stuck to the saddle this time, I'd fucking araldited myself on, he wasn't gunna beat me, I was ready, I stuck to that saddle alright … but hey … why the hell am I sailing through the air then? Something was wrong. I shouldn't be flying through the air, and hang on… I'm still in the fucking saddle!

Something's wrong …something's terribly wrong.
It didn't compute – me … saddle … thin air … no horse!

Then …*KAVOOMPAR*… me and the saddle sprawled out across the dirt in an untidy heap, feeling sorry for ourselves. Shitbags had taken off, he'd probably thought he had actually killed me this time … so I wasn't gunna be much fun anymore.

The four-legged can of Pal had beat me – good and proper.

The head stockman pulls up in an old Toyota laughin' his head off and reckons to have a bit of a rest and then we'll catch him and give it another go.

"You almost had him", he kept sayin, "…you almost had him!"

Well I always have found it hard to talk when I'm severely concussed half-buried in the ground with a saddle on top of me, but I think my reply went somewhere along the lines of "...*You fuckin' ride him!*"

And so thus ended the titanic battle between man and beast and as I got unceremoniously thrown in the back of the Toyota like a sack of spuds, I'm thinkin, 'isn't it great ... in this day and age of rapidly growing technology to still be able to make a dollar sitting on the back of a horse!'

It really is something special.

M E AND ME MATE KYM AND THE TWO GIRLS we'd met
earlier were tipping it down like there was no tomorrow, you
know – slam this ... skull that ... bang this down, bang that down,
people yellin'..

It's Friday night, it's Darwin, it's hot, and it's flowin'.

We're dancing, sweatin', and someone reckons – 'the beach' – next
minute me and Kym are in the back of an old Volkswagon. The two
girls we'd met were in the front and the night was progressing at a
rapid rate. The one driving looked hot, sweaty and pissed, and her
friend next to her looked really hot, really sweaty, and really pissed.
I looked across at Kym. He just looked pissed ... and he wasn't the
Lone Ranger.

Then came the beach and the breeze – relief at last.

Time for a walk... "Yeah, that's the go..."
Next minute one of the girls has got me in a headlock and she's

searching for me lips, but shit, it's hard to be passionate when she's burping up Bundy. And I'm thinkin', 'her B.O. reminded me of a rotting carcass out on the flat.'

But that's grog for you. It will lead you into all sorts of reefy areas.

So we did the business. It wasn't that passionate. Sweat, sand and the night air filled with the tepid aromas of her lingering B.O. Her armpits were lethal weapons. I'm thinkin', 'Shit does this girl use spray or does she just rely on compost?' Well anyway it wasn't a scene from Romeo and Juliet that's for sure. It was a scene from Darwin on a hot Friday night ... pissed and reckless.

Me and Kym finally make it home and the two girls in the Volkswagon roar off into the night. "*Great night ...*" "*Yeah, great night*", we were mumbling to each other as we staggered inside.

'Better brush the teeth', I'm thinkin' '... no too tired. I'll do 'em tomorrow. Time to crash.'

Then the guilt sets in ...

'Oh well, better give 'em a scrape', I thought. So I went to the bathroom to give them a brush and there's Kym washin' his old fella in the basin with soapy water. "Oops sorry mate", I reckoned. Looks like I'll be doin' the teeth tomorrow anyway... Kym's using the basin to wash his old fella... *Eh*! ...Wonder why he's doin that?

Then a scene from the old school days comes flashin' back into my brain and there's the teacher tellin' us kids about social diseases. You know wear this, do that, wash this protect yourself.

'Ah ... that's right, that's the go. Gotta watch out. Maybe I better give mine a scrub', I'm thinkin' ... but too late. I started to drift and sleep got the better of me, and before I knew it, I was choked out.

So the weekend progressed as normal and by Sunday me and Kym were broke, and by Monday it was back to work and the events from the weekend were just blurry memories.

But by Monday arvo it was apparent I'd contracted a little more than just blurry memories.

More flashbacks from school and I could see the teacher again pointing out the symptoms of stuff you really didn't want to know about, and shit it looked like I drew the short straw – you know, it looked like I had something. 'What a shame job', I'm thinkin', and there was no way around it ... it was gunna have to be a trip to the doctor!

Now I knew it was going to be embarrassing. I knew it was gunna be tough, but shit I never expected the doctor to be a woman, and as I walked into the room and seen her, my first reaction was to run off. But what do you do? I wanted to get rid of whatever I had, and she was the only way.

Now this woman doctor was no ordinary woman doctor either.

She was a middle-aged, full on, traditional Indian lady wrapped in all the scarves and garments they wear. She had a red ruby embedded into her forehead, and she was the real thing. It was like being at one of those festivals when everyone is there in national costume. She joined her hands together as if about to pray and welcomed me, and as she spoke her head moved from side to side and I'm thinkin', 'This woman is going to be bloody horrified when I tell her I think I've got a dose.'

I was really feeling a bit of panic comin' on.

So she asked me what seemed to be the problem, and when I finally got out what the problem was she clapped her hands together and looked up to the heavens, her eyeballs rolling around all over the place and she starts to mumble, "*no,no,no,no,no*". And with her eyes still rollin' around in their sockets she reckons "*vedy bard mun... vedy naughty mun... and vedy bard mun... and now you will show it to me!*"

'Oh shit no', I'm thinkin'. This is getting serious. How bloody embarrassing. So there she was, hands clasped together and head going from side to side mumbling: "*You are vedy naughty mun*" ... and there's me having to wop it out.

So she gloved up, and I pulled it out.

She was embarrassed. I was embarrassed. It was a shocker.

She seemed to stalk it for a while as if it was gunna jump up and bite her.

Then she awkwardly goes on with the examination, and then when all that business is over she gets on the phone to the nurse to prepare two injections of whatever. So then she produces a form to fill out, you know ... what was the girl's name? ...her address? ...where did the act take place? ...my relationship with the girl? Now this was just as embarrassing as having to expose my tackle gear and of course I couldn't answer the questions.

   I mean shit, I didn't know the girl's full name or where she lived. I explained what happened: "You know," I'm sayin "...look it was just one of those Friday nights in Darwin. It was hot, we were drunk and we ended up at the beach then it just seemed to happen."

Well off she went – again!

The hands clasped together, she looked up to the heavens, the eyeballs rolled back. "*No,no,no,no,no. Naughty mun and vedy, vedy naughty bard mun,*" she reckoned. I just had me head hung low coppin' it sweet, although the thought of jumping out the window and running off seemed pretty good when all of a sudden the door opens and a nurse walks in with a tray and on it is two of the biggest, most dangerous looking syringes I'd ever seen.

I mean shit they looked like something you'd have used on Phar Lap!

Now the Indian doctor when she seen these things she starts to spark up a bit. This was the bit she was lookin' forward to, you could see it. "*Oh yes, naughty, naughty,*" she reckons as she's eyin' off the syringes. Then it was "*Drop 'em and bend over*", and I think she seen this as some type of punishment, because she just drove 'em home, one in each cheek. And she didn't hold back. It was like getting stabbed in the bum with a filleting knife. She pumped it right into me, giving it that extra twist for good luck, and I'm thinkin' 'now I know how a satay feels.'

So she give me a good ol' skewering and a lecture on *"vedy, vedy appropriate behaviour"* ... then the ordeal was over. I went home and me backside was fairly tender ... you know: a bit saddle sore. So I tell me mate Kym the story and he went into hysterics. I couldn't sit down for days. I just had to lean on things, but I got over it.

I suppose I learnt my lesson. I was lucky because in those days there wasn't the deadly diseases gettin' around, and a shot of penicillin was all that was needed to clear it up.

But shit ... it goes to show you, you just gotta be careful.

So you know next time you're in Darwin, it's Friday night, it's hot and it's flowin', just think about the Indian doctor and the injection fit for a horse, and you just might handle things a bit more cautiously. And like the good old Indian doc reckons *"you must always use - vedy ... vedy ... appropriate behaviour!"*

Collecting Crocodile Eggs

NOW YOU SAY TO YOURSELF, well, 'you'll never catch me doing that' or 'no way mate, I don't have to worry about that because I'll never be doing it.' In general, there's things you just never dream of doing or situations you just didn't figure you'd ever find yourself in. Then one day you wake and there you are, somewhere, doing something that quite frankly was not in the game plan.

Well, I suppose I was put in such a position and not only was it not in the game plan, but it happened to be probably one of the most dangerous occupations around – farming saltwater crocodiles. Not exactly what you'd call 'man's best friend'.

This all took place up in North East Arnhem Land, a beautiful wild and totally unique part of the Northern Territory.

A cousin of mine was working with an aboriginal community up there and he invited me up to have a look around anytime I had the chance.

I'd just finished a little stint at the Bungle Bungle National Park up the top of Western Australia taking people out there on camping trips. It hadn't been a bad number, a little adventure, combined with some great Australian scenery.

All in all, a good stint.

The dry season, which is the time for travelling and exploring this part of the country was now coming to an end and the wet season was coming up, so I weighed things up and decided to move on. The fact that I was working for a complete arsehole also had a bit to do with it I suppose.

Good chance to catch up with my cousin over in Arnhem Land and see a bit of new country I figured. So, after about 19 Emu Bitters at a not so quiet pub in Kununurra, I felt pretty happy and was looking forward to whatever was coming up next – absolutely no idea that in a few short weeks' time, I'd be doin' a Croc Dundee in some swamp in Arnhem Land, but unlike the movie, I'd be doin' me own stunts and the crocs would be real (I mean extremely fuckin' real).

I flew into the township of Nhulunbuy, situated in the top north-east corner of the Northern Territory. No chance of driving there at that time of year as the rivers and creeks were all on the way up with the early rains.

I met up with my cousin who was a likable bloke in his 40's. As per family tradition, he had an esky full of cold beer. So we caught up with each other's yarns and sucked the guts out of a couple of cold ones. He filled me in on the aboriginal community he was involved with, and their projects they had going, one of them being a crocodile farm. 'Great' I thought, 'nothing better than aboriginal people trying to create some type of economic stability for the future', I'm thinkin' as I tore the rip-cord off another Victoria Bitter. My cousin Paul assured me they are a pretty good mob up here. Keen to stay traditional but also keen to hit the 21st century up and running economically.

We drove around as the monsoon rain started to slip down out of incredible shaped clouds and I'm thinkin', 'what a beautiful area, woodlands full of Stringy Bark and Cycad Palms, Pandanus clumped here and there, Ironwood, Woolly Butt, beautiful contrasts of various shades of green against the red ochred earth.' Very easy on the eye... Totally intoxicating, and totally intoxicated we were getting as we drove out in the direction of the community. Paul singing old Dean Martin songs and me just enjoying the scenery.

'What a great little holiday this is gunna be', I'm thinkin'. 'Bit of fishin', bit of drinkin', bit more fishin', no need to do it hard all the time', I said to myself. 'Bloody fan, bloody tastic!'

Now the next few weeks were great, the community was situated on an exquisite part of coastline. Fish everywhere, oysters on the rocks, crabs, clams, mussels, you name it, I ate it. The people there were very friendly and warm and I fitted in pretty good, making friends easy enough and just meandering around the joint.

The Croc farm project seemed to be going OK. There were cages and ponds, incubators and of course, crocs. Mostly ones that had been caught locally and a couple looked pretty toey, just quietly, and you could see where they had been testing the fences trying to bust out ...'I wouldn't want one hangin' off me arse', I'm thinking, as I moseyed around.

Paul was the Operations Manager and there was another white bloke who ran the day to day farm stuff, ably supported by a team of local aboriginal blokes from the community.

As Paul pointed out, the farm was really geared up as a nursery. That means, they planned to collect croc eggs from the wild, incubate them and when they hatched, grow them up a little, then sell them to other farms, like a supplier of crocodiles.

'That's great', I thought, 'but what dickhead would go out in the swamps and floodplains of Arnhem Land and try and steal eggs from a pissed off clucky croc?'

You'd never see that one advertised at Centrelink, that's for sure.

Well, anyway, a couple of weeks went on. I dragged a few more coral trout onto the coals, ate about eighty dozen more oysters, a la naturale and enjoyed the odd cleansing ale or three.

Life was pretty good alright. The sun went up, the sun went down and usually with splashes of intense colour, stretching like pastel fingers across the sky, turning all sorts of shades. Totally breathtaking. I was turning into a beach bum and loving it.....

'Who'd be crazy enough to collect croc eggs. You'd have to be mad', I'm thinkin', as I filleted my first barramundi for the day. 'What a joke.'

Two mudcrabs and a panikan of billy tea later, old Paul rocks up in a cloud of dust, and gets out of his Toyota in a fluster and tells me he's had a fall out with the croc farm manager and the croc farm manager's done the 'Harold Holt'.

"Shit, that's no good", I said, "do you want a hand?" Well, Paul reckoned that would be great, that would give him time to find another manager.

So, for the next couple of weeks, I was acting Croc Farm Manager. No big deal, just keeping everything alive and fed, and joining in with the aboriginal workers. Just keeping the joint going.

Now, as usual, I went at it pretty hard, really getting stuck into the place, cleaning it up, making the garden look good, mowed all the weeds and feedin' the crocs up.

I really hit it off with the boys working there, as well. I love animals and have got a good head for that sort of stuff.

Now, maybe it was destiny, maybe it was fate...

Or just maybe and more likely, they couldn't find anyone else!

But everyone was unanimous – they wanted me to stay on and run the farm.

Now I can't resist a good challenge. All through my adult life, I've been in many situations where my brain is saying, 'look for Christ sake, tell them to piss off, don't do it', but my mouth always seems to say "yeah, no worries, I'll have a go at that." Usually I end up into it up to my neck.

This was no different. Me brain lost out again and off I went.

Phil O'Brien, Croc Farmer! That's really got a great ring to it, I'm thinkin', yep, no doubt about it, it's got a great ring. Very important, very official, very distinguished. Of course I didn't exactly realise what the whole thing entailed, and I completely forgot the bit about collecting eggs in the wild. I was just swept away by the glory of the whole thing.

I envisaged that in years to come, there would be three names synonymous with crocodiles, Paul Hogan, Linda Koslowski and Phil O'Brien!

Yep, life was good. The sun came up and the sun went down. No problems.

Now it had only been a week or so after my inauguration and things were going great guns. Plans to do this, plans for that and so on... then the word come down the line, 'meeting under the Banyan tree' at dinner time. No worries. Me being the new crocodile farm manager and all that, I could fit that into my schedule, no problems. A bit of official business. Yep, I'll strut down there in all my croc farming glory, no sweat... I might even have a bit of input, seeing I was an important person.

Well, there we were, under the Banyan tree, me, Paul, the operations manager, the head bloke of the tribe and a few other men.

Time to go for eggs. "The Baru (crocodile) will be nesting now. Now is the time", said the leader.

No problem, everyone agreed.

Me thinking, 'who's the dumb prick gunna be that goes and gets them, poor bugger', I'm thinkin', 'poor bastard.' Maybe they're gunna fly 'Evil Kenevil' in from America or something, I joked to myself. No one else would do something so crazy.

Well, great stuff I pipe up, let's fill those incubators with eggs and get this show on the road... all full of piss and wind.

Then Paul turned to me and said, in a tone of voice similar to a judge passing sentence, "get organised Phil, we'll have a chopper coming from Katherine later this week and you and Stewy can head out and start collecting."

'Start collecting?... start collecting, fuckin what?', I'm thinkin'. "Fuckin hey, are you talking to me?"

I looked around, fuck ... he was!

Yep... I was the man alright. Good old Phil. Great guy, top bloke. But a gator got him ... I can see the headstone now.
Me brain tried to cut in with 'pull out, pull out, it's not too late', but unfortunately my lips had already formed the syllables – "yeah, no worries, I'll have a go at that."

Now stealing eggs from crocs is probably on par with going over Niagara Falls in a 44-gallon drum. Theoretically, it's possible to survive, but if you don't make it, no one would be really surprised, you know, life would go on and you'd just end up as croc shit, floating down the river, no problem.

'I'm fairly in it now', I'm thinkin', 'fairly in it...'

Stewy, my partner in all this, was a full blood aboriginal bloke, in his 30's. A likable bloke, his job was to look out for the mum, while I got the eggs out of the nest. No worries, no sweat, only one problem... we weren't going to take a gun, as the crocodile was a sacred totem to the people there. To shoot one, wouldn't go down real well, so our protection was a 14-foot wooden paddle off someone's boat – great!

It's coming together real well...

To put the icing on the cake, the Conservation Commission of the Northern Territory, wanted me to fill out a questionnaire at every croc nest I found, as they were trying to gather data on crocodiles. Questions such as, what grass was the nest compiled of? How many eggs?, Was the female present? Was she aggressive? The temperature, and so on...

How does a bloke do all this with a croc tearing at his jugular, I'm trying to work out. I think they thought I was Mandrake the Magician or something.

Well anyway, there was no turning back now, and like I always say 'I can't resist a good challenge'.

So me and Stewy spent the next few days dropping 44's of aviation fuel in various locations out bush as the chopper only had two hours flying time on a tank. We got hold of some maps of various river systems and worked out which places we'd try out. Stewy really knew this area well – and we marked down places he already knew where crocs nested. Virtually all the nesting areas were inaccessible by vehicle. That was the reason for hiring the helicopter.

The quota they were aiming at, was 2000 eggs.

A croc will lay anywhere between 20 to 60 eggs, so, it would have to be a really big effort to find enough nests to reach the target. This little project was definitely not one for the faint hearted, and although I turned out to be the silly bugger going out to collect the eggs, I really wanted this to work for the community.

The helicopter finally arrived flying all the way across from Katherine. The pilot was a good sort of bloke, named Mick , or Mick Dundee as he was nicknamed...

He introduced himself as Mick followed by "and this is David", clutching at a knife hanging off his belt, which was actually, in size, more like a sword. You meet all sorts of characters in these remote places, there's no doubt about it. I'd actually heard of Mick before and he had a good reputation as a pilot and prided himself on being pretty reliable. Between him and David, there wasn't much they couldn't handle.

Me, Mick and Stewy hit it off pretty well and we planned our strategy for the following day, which, by the way, was a Friday and there's an old bush superstition, never start anything on a Friday.

'What the hell', I thought – 'probably wouldn't be coming back in one piece anyway.'

Our plan was to fly low over the Peter John Floodplain and the neighbouring Cato River spotting the nests from the air. Then Mick would drop me and Stewy as close as he could to the nest. It all depended on how many trees and the type of bush that was around, as to how close he could get with the chopper. If it was open ground, we were sweet, if it wasn't, we'd have to hike in from wherever Mick could land.

The next day, the sun came up and I wondered what I would be doing when it went down again hopefully hangin' off a cold can and not going through the digestive system of some potential belt and matching handbag! Mick Dundee was up at first light servicing the chopper. Which, incidentally, had a pretty wild paint job. Something like Bob Dylan would have flown around in, back in the 70's.

So there we were – me, Stewy and Mick. All set. Nostrils flarin' ready for the big day. I had me steal cap boots on specially, at least me toes were protected.

Our equipment was secured, two large eskies to put the eggs in, the 14-foot paddle for protection, a water container and a pack of Arnotts Family Assortment shoved under the seat.

Mick kicked her in the guts and off we choppered...

I actually hate flying, but a helicopter's something else. Especially flying as low as what Mick was doing. Across the bay we flew, going that low, I was thinking I should have brought a hand line and some bait. We finally crossed the bay and headed out across the treetops. The country opening up beneath. It was so exhilarating, I forgot all about my fear of flying. The scenery was magic.

A bit further on, and we hit the flood plain country that pans out from the Peter John River. Flocks of Brolga, Magpie Geese, Egrets, Jabiru and Water Buffalo that fat, they could hardly raise a trot.

Mick was backing off with the throttle a bit, as a likely bit of country came into view. Sure enough, there was a nest – a mound of about one meter high and three or four meters around, grass and mud raked up and packed together working like compost, generating just the right amount of heat to incubate the eggs deep inside. We were lucky, as the nest was out in the open and Mick could land quite close.

From the air, the flood plain grass only looked about a foot long, but once you actually got down amongst it, it was well over your waist and in some areas, well over your head. So Stewy was first out with the paddle poking it around in front of him like a mine detector. I had an esky and a clipboard complete with Conservation Commission data sheets and thermometer.

We got to the nest fairly easy – the female wasn't to be seen, but her tracks were everywhere and you could bet she wasn't far away.

There was plenty of tension, Stewy raking the grass with the paddle. I started to break apart the nest. I got to the eggs and started taking the temperature and checking them out. I looked up at Stewy, who by now was leaning on the paddle, rolling a smoke. Not a problem in the world.

I slowly took each egg out and placed them in the esky, packing them in with some of the nest material. How the croc lays them, is how they have to stay for the 80 days or so of incubation. No twisting or turning the eggs. So I put a mark with a pencil on the top of each egg, so we knew which way was up. A slow process.

With the eggs finally packed in the esky, we headed back to the chopper, climbed in and gave Mick the thumbs up, and off we went looking for another one. 'This wasn't going to be that hard', I thought, and what great scenery. No problem, no sweat... too easy.

It wasn't long and we spotted another one, this time it was in amongst some trees. So Mick dropped us a few hundred metres away in a clearing.

Off we went again, Stewy with his paddle, me with the esky and clipboard, 'piece of piss', I'm thinkin', 'piece of piss.'

Pushing through the long grass in the direction of the nest... so far, no sweat. But things started to get sticky... we hit a bit of lush rain forest type stuff, vines everywhere and it was very hard to see any distance, as the bush was quite thick. To make it worse, the ground was getting really boggy and I was starting to get a little bit of a twitch around the old clacker valve walking in slush up to my knees. Stewy was skimming through it all right as he didn't weigh a real lot.

We could see the nest finally in a bit of a clearing. So far, no croc... so I thought we were home and hosed. When about ten meters from the nest, I hit a pocket of real soft stuff and sunk straight down up to my neck and I'll be buggered if I could move. Stewy was skimming along in front like a mudskipper totally unaffected, but then again, I would have been nearly double his weight.

I was feeling a little nervous with just me head sticking out of the mud like some type of hors d'oeuvre. 'If the mum bolted out of somewhere right now, I'd be stuffed', I'm thinkin', 'she'd just bite me head clean off and say thanks for comin'.'

You know, it's times like these you are meant to see your life flash before your eyes, but I closed my eyes and all I could see was a Jatz biscuit with an olive sitting on top of it. Funny about that...

Stewy doubled back and after a few grunts and groans, he managed to pull me out. I grabbed the esky and we forged on to the nest, me feeling slightly rattled and covered in shit.

The PH level of my arse had risen considerably.

I started the slow process of getting the eggs out and I heard a sound like someone blowing bubbles in the water... so I spun around and there was a croc... no more than about four or five meters away. It must have been laying doggo in what looked like a shallow pool of muddy water. The croc must have decided enough was enough and it looked like it was getting ready to do some serious chompin'.

Stewy went to belt it in the snout – but the croc just exploded out of the water, grabbed the paddle, shredding the end of it and flung it out of Stewy's hands. It went flying into the long grass. This all took about half of a second. The power and speed of the croc was unbelievable.

Stewy backed up, turned to me with a look on his face that reminded me of Michael Jackson just about to sing 'Thriller!'

He started yelling *"mudgenna, mudgenna"* which is aboriginal for "let's split the scene pronto." So without too much ado, we vacated, making sure to avoid the real muddy spot as it wasn't a real good time to get stuck.

The croc held its ground, jaws wide open, letting out an evil hissing sound.

We regrouped and went and got the 14-foot paddle which was now 12 and a half-foot, with a frayed end and headed back into the fight. We had no choice. The esky was still there next to the nest and we'd only got half of the eggs out. Stewy mumbling *"yaka myanmuk"* which translated means, "it's getting very hot in the fuckin' kitchen." To his credit, Stewy was solid as a rock and he never looked like folding.

Back we went. Stewy got a good one in early off, which stunned the croc, but once again she got hold of the paddle, this time rolling her body, flinging the solid wooden oar into the long grass again. She then flew straight for us. Jaws gaped wide open. Stewy came out the blocks lookin' like Jesse Owens set to break the Olympic long jump record in Berlin in 1936 and I wasn't far behind. Conservation Commission data sheets flyin everywhere, I just had time to tick, YES, THE FEMALE WAS PRESENT, and grab the esky.

Off we went me and Stewy flying through the long grass with the croc hot on the case.....but luckily for us, she stopped once we were clear of the nest area. Me and Stewy agreeing that round two went clearly to the croc.

We found the wooden oar which now had been reduced to 11 foot and very splintered at one end. We headed back to the chopper.

This was pretty well how it was for the next week, flying, landing, mud, bush, crocs exploding out of all sorts of places, laughing, running, flying, landing, crocs lunging and moments of spectacular scenery and of course – moments of sheer terror.

Top: Mick 'Dundee' and Stewy with the anti-croc pole.
Bottom: Stewy bravely pushes through the elephant grass at Arafura Swamp

I wouldn't have missed it: NO WAY. But by the end of a solid week of it, I felt like I'd just returned from a stint on the Kokoda Trail.

The 14-foot paddle was down to 6 foot and showing signs of cracking. We'd collected about 1000 eggs and had them incubating away at the croc farm. A pretty good effort, not quite the 2000 we'd hoped for, but still, no one had been injured and me, Mick and Stewy had really bonded together well.

Anyway, the word come down the line, 'meeting under the Banyan tree' at lunchtime... no worries, no sweat. We thought we were probably going to get a pat on the back or a medal or something.

Me and Stewy marched down as if it was an Anzac Day Parade. Very proud.

You know there's nothing like being in a life and death situation for forging solid friendships. So proudly we arrived at the Banyan tree ready for all the accolades that no doubt we would probably be receiving.

Well... I couldn't have been more wrong. Someone had come up with the really terrific idea of going out again for more eggs. This time to a place called Arafura Swamp.

Now Arafura Swamp was over towards central Arnhem Land and I'm thinkin' 'you couldn't have found a more out of the way place if you sat down and dedicated your life to it.'

Mick Dundee, who reckoned he knew that area, piped up and said "great lizard country, bloody good lizard country." And believe me, I don't think he was talking about fucking geckos either! But from what he was saying, the terrain would be a lot tougher and even more dangerous than what we'd already been through.

The main reason being, the great abundance of what they call, elephant grass. It grows around billabongs and waterways and it's that high and thick, you can lean on it and it can support a bloke's weight without even bending. You can imagine trying to hike through the shit...

I felt like I'd just done two tours of duty in Vietnam and now they're asking me to do another one. But sure enough, me lips formed those syllables: "no worries, I'll have a go at that." So off we went.

Two days later, we were chopperin' into Arafura Swamp with a new 14-foot wooden oar strapped to the skid of the helicopter. Mick got hold of an old revolver. It looked like he'd borrowed it from John Wayne. It was shoved under the seat next to the Arnotts Family Assortment. He thought a bit of insurance was in order...

Spirits were high as we came in low over the Paperbarks and if I thought the Peter John Floodplain was pretty, this place was absolutely exquisite.

There was a real abundance of water birds.

'Well, at least everything will be well fed', I'm thinkin'...

We started scanning the area looking for a nest. We didn't have to go far and there it was, a classic croc nest right on the edge of a bit of swamp surrounded by elephant grass and heaps of it. 'This was gunna be a real prick', I'm thinkin'.

Mick landed about 150 meters from the nest. Unfortunately, that was as close as he could get.

Mick decided to come with us this time – donning a Panama hat looking very Jungle Jim. Stewy arming himself with the wooden paddle and after a small discussion on how this elephant grass was definitely gunna give everyone the screaming shits, we headed off.

The going was slow and hard, as we'd figured. Stewy actually having to rest the paddle on the grass, then walk up the paddle a meter or so and then repeat the process, as it was that dense.

We would have been roughly half way to the nest, maybe another 50 or 60 meters to go, when all of a sudden, the elephant grass up ahead was just crashing down as if something was charging through it. Something big....and it was coming our way.

CRASH, CRASH, BANG, CRASH, CRASH, WHOOSH.

It all happened so quick. None of us had time to say or do anything. Before we knew it, the grass parted directly in front of us and out emerged the wildest, ugliest, blackest outright baddest looking croc I'd ever seen and it was right on us.

Stewy tried to reverse up, but backed into me and I went flying back into Mick. As a result, we all went arse up – it was sort of a domino type of effect.

So we all hit the deck, legs and arms going everywhere, like the Three Stooges doing a bit of slap stick. The croc could have grabbed any one of us. It was that close, I could smell its breath. It had black weed hanging off its head and a full set of black, slimy looking teeth and it was pissed off. Its jaws gaped wide open. It wasn't about to break into a verse of 'Love me Tender' by Elvis either. It was there to do some bone crushing.

The whole thing happened so quick, it was almost surreal.

Mick was the only one that showed any real initiative and he decided to head west. He was up and out of there, and I mean, he was smokin'. He hit the elephant grass that hard, I swear I could see the imprint of his body just like in the cartoons when someone goes through a wall or something.

He powered through the bush like the Six Million Dollar man just after a tune up, stridin' right out. Me and Stewy should have been with him, but we were still on the ground virtually nose to nose with the croc, not exactly sure which way we should play it. The croc sizing us up, I knew if I stayed there any longer, I would have soiled my strides and I'm pretty sure, Stewy already had. So we slowly backed away and got out of there.

We regrouped back at the chopper, a little rattled. We all agreed to try plan B, which was, try and scare it off with the helicopter. This will do it we all reckoned. So we took off and spotted the croc, Mick trying to buzz it with the chopper. The croc was lunging up and snapping, totally undaunted by the size and noise of the helicopter. It just seemed to make it more annoyed.

'There's no doubt about it – this thing's possessed', I'm thinkin'.

Plan B wasn't getting us anywhere, so we landed and it looked like we'd have to try Plan C. Plan C was basically, grab the John Wayne memorial revolver from under the seat and head back in.

Now, Plan C didn't exactly go over that well with everyone, especially Stewy. He was all for Plan D, which was piss off and go somewhere else, preferably back home.

But in true Aussie fighting tradition, we marched back in... we had no intentions of killing it, but at least we might be able to scare it. Maybe give it one around the tail or something, just to piss it off out the way, so we could get to the nest.

Into the grass we went... it was easier this time as we'd already knocked a bit of a track down the first time. We got to the site of the previous ambush and no sign of the monster, so we picked up the paddle and the stuff that got left there, and pushed on. We took the trail that the croc had made, working our way along. Senses working overtime, expecting at any moment the shit to hit the fan again.

You could really feel the tension in the air. You could also smell it in the air, as I think Stewy gave one a bit too much choke.

So on we pushed, bit by bit, no talking. This was no joke. Everyone concentrating, crouching low, pushing through the grass.

The trail ended and we found ourselves at the nest.

No croc.

Then up out the water about 20 yards away, it raised it's awesome, grotesque, weed ridden head and let out a real guttural groan. It started swimming in towards us. Stewy mumbled, something that sounded like "*yo narma*" which, in English, means roughly, "hasta la vista, baby." Then he opened up with the John Wayne Memorial and to my surprise, the antique actually worked... He fired a few shots around her head to try and frighten her off.

Phil takes the temperature of a croc's nest at Arafura Swamp...
whilst Stewy puts a few over the Mum's head

We seemed to have her bluffed. She stayed in the water just groaning her head off.

So, Mick and myself got the eggs out as quick as we could.

Just as we thought things were sweet, the croc made another charge through the water and Stewy lined the gun up, pulled the trigger... Nothing – we were out of bullets ... shit! Stewy yelled something that sounded like "GOONA MOONA SUCK ACHOONA", which translated means roughly: "FUCK THIS!"

So we grabbed the gear and we floated, this time it was us crashing through the elephant grass – and we didn't look back until we reached the chopper!

Now, this little drama sort of set the precedent for Arafura Swamp. There were plenty more little escapades and narrow escapes, stand-offs and takeoffs, but we somehow got through it, Stewy being a real credit to his people and Mick being, not only a good pilot, but a good bloke to work with. And I think it brought the best out in all of us.

We got our quota of 2000 eggs for the farm and we sure did it the hard way.

But then again– I don't think there really was an easy way!

The Kiss of the Kangaroo

KISSING A KANGAROO WAS THE LAST THING I thought I'd be doing later that night, no doubt about it. I mean, if someone would have asked me earlier on: "What do you think you'll be doin' later?"

Well hey – I don't think I would have replied: "Oh well, probably kissing a kangaroo." You know what I mean.

It's in the same category as getting abducted by aliens. Logically thinking it shouldn't ever happen. I mean that's what you'd reckon.

Well, you know a funny thing happened to me a while back.

I was driving back to a little gold mine in central western Australia, pretty remote sort of place. I was working out there and I'd just had a week off down in town so as per usual I'd played it pretty hard.

I was feelin' a bit rough so I was pretty well looking forward to getting back out bush to sort of piece me-self back together again.

Me stomach was a little tender after the severe tequila slamming it got the night before and the old nerves were pretty shot. I mean I wasn't exactly displaying the reflexes of an Israeli Jet Fighter Pilot either as I poked along in the old ute.

I came around this sweeping bend and 'oh shit' wouldn't you know it. A bunch of about ten kangaroos, the big red variety, had decided to hold a meeting right in the middle of the road.

Before I knew it I was right in amongst them.

The bush on each side of the road was really dense so they had nowhere to go but down the road. So there we all are, charging down the road, me tryin' to slow down and dodge roos jumping around everywhere. It must have been a reflex action or something but I went to stick my head out of the driver's side window to have a look as it was a pretty dark night, not much moon.

It was a million to one.

I looked out just as this Big Red that was bounding along next to the ute decided he'd look in!

And Smack Bang Slurp and *Wamo*! The roo's lips met mine in a clash of fur, beard, teeth and believe it or not tongue! Good grief... Well, I really didn't need that.

So I reefed the wheel to 'port' and ran straight off the road into the bush, skidding around all over the turnout, nearly losing it. The roos bolted past heading for open country and were really high tailing it with one particular roo way out in front, doin' ninety, ears pinned right back.

Shaking my head I'm wondering: 'What the f*&@!'

Was I just attacked by a 'gay roo' or what?

I got out the car somewhat dazed and walked around a bit.

I needed some first aid, so after a quick check of the car I reached in and grabbed an emergency can of beer I had stashed in the glove box. I took a swill and gazed up at the stars wondering who the hell's gunna believe this?

And I'm thinkin', 'shit, a bloke could need a little counselling after this one!'

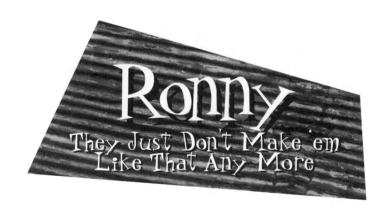

Ronny

They Just Don't Make 'em Like That Any More

I FIRST MET RON WHEN I'D STARTED WORKING for this safari tour mob in Darwin. This particular company handled mainly overseas tourists and offered a range of camping tours to places such as Kakadu National Park. Ronny was the best and most experienced guide they had, so me being the new boy, the company figured it would be a good idea to tag along with Ron on one of his tours to get orientated, and pick up a few tips off the master.

Now Ron had one of the most colourful histories of any bloke I'd ever met, and whichever way you look at it I don't think there were too many dull moments in old Ronny's life, that's for sure.

As a young bloke, he served in the British Navy in World War Two before coming out to Australia. It didn't take long and Ron found himself taking to the Australian bush as if he was born and bred for it. He became a stockman, and later on a drover of some repute before a twist of fate found him fighting in the Korean War ... actually it wasn't really a twist of fate. Ron being a bit of a lad in his younger days rode his horse into a pub in Katherine – for a laugh.

Well it seemed like a good idea at the time.
Once inside the pub the horse decided to go mad and proceeded to kick the living shit out of everything inside. This included tables, chairs, people, mirrors, bottles, doors, windows and a few more people!

And in true Territory tradition Ron never shifted from the saddle.

Well anyway the Katherine police front up and there's a slight altercation and there's a few knockouts, and Ronny's having the time of his life but for some reason the local constabulary didn't quite take it too well. And they presented Ronny with two very interesting options.

"It's like this Ron", they reckon ... "the Army's looking for blokes to go to Korea, and Fannie Bay Gaol is looking for blokes as well. What's it gunna be?"

Not a lot to choose from here, but Ron opted for Korea. And once again Ron found himself in another war, and Korea was no picnic either. He saw a lot of things he'd pretty well rather forget about. And on returning to Australia the bush once again embraced him, and over the forthcoming years Ron went on to really create a name for himself in outback Australia.

He was tough and he was hard, but always quick with a joke and a laugh. He possessed the staunch principles and manners of a generation of fair dinkum Australians that evolved from a tough, honest part of our history. The clichéd phrase, 'They don't make 'em like that any more' has never rung so true. Ron always took things as they came. As far as he was concerned you were innocent till proven guilty and he'd give anyone a fair go. But if crossed Ronny could really deal it out if he had to.

One old mate of mine that knew Ron reckoned, the only way to stop Ron when he was in full flight would be to cut off his head. Fortunately Ronny took a lot of provoking to really crank up.

In the seventies when the Top End flood plains were full of water buffalo Ron got hold of a fair piece of country and built himself a meatworks, and for years was a big player in the Buffalo Industry, exporting Buff meat around Australia and then overseas. Ron would spend many a day hunting buffalo out on the flood plains, and with 100 bullets Ron could drop 101 buffalo ... now that's providing the last two were standing close together.

But the era of the buffalo came and it went in the Northern Territory, and Ronny decided it was time to take on the biggest, the most dangerous and the most nerve racking challenge of his life ... no, not hunting crocodiles or buffalo, no, not breaking in wild horses or fighting in wars, no ... something even more terrifying. Yep – you guessed it – dealing with the general public!

Ronny became a tour guide.

Now Ron knew every bird, billabong, hill, every tree, and every Aboriginal rock painting and green ant nest in the Top End. He was missin' a few teeth and a few fingers but Ronny was still a warrior, and he was a genuine slice of the outback and people loved to be around him. In his blue singlet and caved in old hat, Ronny would hike mile after mile up and down through the rugged splendour of Kakadu, and if you were good enough to keep up Ron would show you the world. If you weren't, he'd simply pick you up on the way back.

For a bloke his age Ron was extremely fit, and no one loved the bush more than he did.

As far as the tourists went he could pretty well do no wrong, you know. When it was dinner time Ronny would just throw a few chops out on a plate and say ... "If you want a chop – cook it." Well, they loved his rugged attitude. If Ron got them up at four in the morning and told them to go and sit on an ant's nest ... they'd do it. And they'd still say what a great bloke Ronny was!

Ron had 'em on a string.

Although, I think there was the odd time things got a bit sticky – like the one night Ron was quietly snoring away under the stars and one Dutch lady gets up and decides to split the whisker. It was a dark night, no moon.

She didn't see Ronny laying there and proceeded to urinate in very close proximity to his head. I think this rattled him a bit, but except for the odd incident, Ron's tours were always successful.

So one Sunday morning about six o'clock me and Ron had teamed up. Ronny was the Legend, and I was the Apprentice. There we were fumbling around in the half dark trying to get the gear ready for this four day camping safari of Kakadu. We were running late and we had ten American tourists to pick up, and me being young and inexperienced, I'm startin' to panic and I look across at Ron and I reckon: "Shit, we're gunna be late Ron." Well Ron casually looked up, slowly took a bite from his apple and matter of factly said: "*Well ... fuck 'em.*"

Ron was not only a settling influence, but sometimes he was a man of few words as well.

So we eventually rounded everyone up from their respective motels and headed off Kakadu bound. It wasn't a bad group – a few of your cigar smoking office type, a young couple, an older couple and a lovely middle-aged lady who apparently was a psychologist.

Ronny blasting through the outer suburbs of Darwin rattling off a few statistics – everyone very excited.

Once we were clear of civilisation we stopped a few times, Ron pointing out various things of interest. Then we called into the old 'Bark Hut Inn' for some smoko. Over a coffee Ron gave me a little piece of advice. He reckoned I was being too nice to everyone. He pointed out that if you start off a tour too nice, everyone expects you to be nice the whole trip ... but he said, "*You should be like me – I start off a grumpy old prick, but anything after that's a bonus for 'em.*"

Ronny: not just your average rough diamond

Ron in his own articulate way hit the nail on the head, and I could see from the onset there was a lot to learn from a seasoned campaigner like Ron.

So off we went rattlin' around Kakadu - me, Ronny and the ten Americans, and the first day went really well. Some great scenery, a look at some age-old rock art, and in the cool of the afternoon we set up camp.

Ronny sizzlin' up a few chops and tellin' yarns, the group loved him. I think as far as they were concerned Ron was the genuine 'Crocodile Dundee' and I don't reckon they were far off either.

That night the mozzies came in fierce, as they often do in that part of the country, and they ripped it into everyone, and in the morning we all were a bit jaded, all except for Ron of course. He had skin like riding boot leather, and never felt a thing. So Ronny's as chirpy as hell after eight great hours of sleep, and it was all go. There just wasn't enough hours in the day for a bloke like Ron – waterfalls to see, billabongs to swim in, and later that day Ron decided we'd do a six kilometre hike straight uphill and down dale to see if the group was fit enough to handle the 12 kilometre hike he planned for the next day.

Ron found the hill he had in mind and then it was onwards and upwards. One of the cigar smoking Americans reckoned: "*Rarny ... Rarny ... why do we have to climb this damn hill, Rarny?*"

Well Ron spins around, clenches his fists and reckons: "Cause it's here," and off he went stridin' right out. Ronny's legs were in four wheel drive and he wasn't lookin' back.

Ronny didn't give a rat's toss bag. The hills were for climbing.

But once on top, although the group were near collapse, the rewards were great. The views were spectacular and to see the Aboriginal rock art that Ron knew was up there was well worth the effort.

For a bloke in his sixties Ron had the constitution of a Brahman bull, and he could go all day. Unfortunately the same couldn't be said about me and the group, and by the time we all got back to camp we were well and truly stuffed.

But the sun wasn't quite down yet.

So Ronny suggests before he goes and kicks the lid off the esky and slings a few chops around: "Why don't we have a bit of a cool off down at this billabong."

Well... everyone reckons it's a great idea, so we grab our towels and we head off down this track leading to this waterhole. It wasn't far and in we go, and it was beautiful, washing the sweat off, enjoying the crystal clear water – everyone relaxing ... well ... that was everyone except Ronny and the charming American psychologist Kathleen. They disappear over a hill ... Ron's wheeled her.

So I start doin' a bit of thinkin', and it's all startin' to add up. It started to add up all right... Earlier that day I noticed that every time Kathleen came near Ron he'd start spinning off the botanical name of every living thing in a ten mile radius – just tryin' to sugar her up a bit. And I think it was working.

You know ... Ronny wasn't just your average rough diamond.

Kathleen was obviously taken by him – well, it was either that or Ronny's got her over the hill showin' her a couple of frogs or some bush tucker or something. Anyway, it wasn't any of my business. I was just the apprentice.

So as the sun slowly disappeared and the lights went out on the escarpment country of Kakadu, me and the group meandered back to camp. What a day.

Soon after, Kathleen and Ronny turn up, Kathleen with a grin from ear to ear and Ron looking very sheepish, and I'm thinkin' 'people don't glow like that after checkin' out a few frogs – no way.'

I think there was some very discreet little liaison going on here ... Ron had transformed himself from the rugged outdoor type to the 'Sheik from Scrubby Creek', and he was sweeping her off her feet, nothing surer.

Later that night I noticed Kathleen drag her swag up close to

Ronny's, and I'm thinkin' 'either Ron's pointing out the Southern Cross or else they're really enjoying each other's company.' And you didn't have to complete Year 12 at Prince Alfred College to work out it was probably the latter.

The next morning Ron's up at sparrow fart galloping around the camp like a young horse on oats, his top lip curled right back. Ron was keen to get out there.

If there was one thing he hated... it was burning good daylight!

So after a quick breakfast of chops á la Ronny we hit the trail. This was the big day because today we were exploring the gorge country of Southern Kakadu – Ron's favourite area. And as the day unfolded, I could see why. It was just one glorious panorama after the next. We swam, we climbed, and we staggered through mile after mile of fantastic rugged Kakadu, Ronny power walking out in front and me and the group wandering behind in various stages of exhaustion.

It was like a scene from the Burma Railway, but somehow Ron had taken us through the pain barrier. We all saw so much and I learnt so much, and with every botanical name that Ronny rattled off, Kathleen would just melt – Ron had won a heart.

That night back at camp spirits were really high, everyone nursing blisters and tending sunburn after the big day. Ron slam dunked a few chops and we all talked about what a great adventure we'd had.

You see, Ronny pointed out there's two ways you can attack a tour... you can go drink coffee and sit around some visitors' centres looking at displays all day, or else you can get out there and really feel the country, and get something out of it.

Although everyone was totally rooted, the group was unanimous it had been a time they'd never forget – a trip of a lifetime.

The old swag called and I was quite happy to lay me bones down that night. Ron and Kathleen had joined their swags together to form a type of cocoon, and as it was the last night I think Ronny wanted to make sure Kathleen knew where the Southern Cross was...

Next day we rolled back into Darwin, everyone a little melancholy the whole thing was coming to an end. Ron was gunna "style up" big time and shout Kathleen a pizza, and after I dropped everyone off to their motels I was heading out to find a book on the botanical names of plants – I mean it obviously worked for Ron.

For me it had been a great apprenticeship into the tour game. I kicked on, and was almost a successful tour guide, only occasionally getting the arse.

Kathleen moved to the Northern Territory and married Ron.

And as far as I know, Ronny's still walking around out there somewhere discovering country people never even knew existed. And like I said earlier ...

"They just don't make 'em like that any more!"

WORKING AS A TOUR GUIDE FOR A WHILE really had its advantages. It was damn hard work but you'd meet people from all over the world, and although things didn't always go as planned, I can confidently say there was never a dull moment. And over time you start to work out the mannerisms of the different nationalities you're dealing with. For example:

Take these three Japanese girls. Butter wouldn't melt in their mouths. They were so friendly and chirpy, and probably a little flirtatious, but this is where you have to be careful...

You have to stay professional, you know – you're on the job. You gotta stay focussed. It doesn't matter what the situation looks like, the golden rule has always been: '*Don't fuck the freight*'. Now as crude as that sounds it does make sense.

OK. Sometimes you hook up and its fun, but more often than not you can get yourself in the shit, and totally spoil a good tour. It all boils down to experience and commonsense.

And as usual, I have to find out things the hard way.

The particular four day camping tour with the Japanese girls started off great. We left Darwin and had a fantastic first day, the girls having the time of their lives, giggling and smiling very affectionately every time I said anything. I mean ... I could show them anything and they loved it. They'd just look up at me and flutter their little Japanesey eyelashes. But hey – no point crackin half a Rajah!

One shouldn't get too excited because that's just how Japanese people are – they just come across very friendly. Now it doesn't mean they want to get romantic. It doesn't even mean they like you. It's just that they're a very respectful, friendly mob, and that's their custom.

Well we camped the first night at this pretty little place called Annaburroo Billabong and were into a few cold ones. The full moon came up in style and we were havin' a good ol' time. I was singin' a few on the guitar and doin' a bit of guzzlin', and the Japanese girls were sipping away and giggling – just embracing the moment. The girls English was very good so communication was no problem. Then the idea came up to have a swim in the moonlight ... no worries. So we put our cozzies on and in we go, me being a little charged up by this time.

So we splashed around and I'm startin' to get swept away by the moment.

You know ... under the stars ... the scent of paperbarks in blossom and the sounds of flying foxes moving through the night, and three Japanese girls dog paddling around all over the joint. For a minute there I forgot I was on the job. I let my guard down.

The flesh became weak.

Next minute one of the Japanese girls pulls in next to me and before I knew it I'd tried to lay a big wet Northern Territory pash fair on her... It was just a reflex action. It could have happened to anyone!

Well, that was it. The curtain came down, the show was over, and I'm very sorry to announce this story doesn't have a very happy ending. There was a definite mood swing with the Japanese girls.

The next three days of the tour were hell.
The Japanese girls made out they couldn't understand any English at all, and they only spoke Japanese to each other. They treated me with contempt. Actually the only word I understood over the next three long days was when I dropped them back in Darwin, and they all reckoned: *"Sayonara."*

Now I'm pretty sure that's Japanese for "Piss off!"

WHEN I REALLY THINK ABOUT IT, my form with women over the years has been really quite dismal. It's like a racing syndicate that buys a horse and pins all their hopes on it, you know, it comes from a good bloodline, looks good in the paddock, has all the right moves – but just never seems to win a race.

Frustrating - yes!
　　Confusing - yes it sure is!
　　　　Depressing - fuckin' oath it can be!

OK, well fair enough there's nights when you're out on the town and you meet some woman and you end up letting the ferret out for a run – well that's great. But it's usually because she's just as desperate as what you are.

When it comes to the ones that really count, you know that 'special girl', you can always depend on old 'No-style' O'Brien to completely blow it. I never seem to get past go. A relationship to me was something that happened to these two people in a movie I saw once at the pictures. I sure as shit wasn't having too many of them. Although a little while back I probably could have done alright for myself if only I'd played my cards right. A little warning here, if you're prone to depression, maybe you better not read the rest of this story...

You know, when this certain girl smiled, she lit the whole place up, it was like she was hooked up to mains power. If you had put a volt meter on her she would have been puttin' out 240 – no worries. Her skin was coffee brown and she had the most beautiful eyes, deep and dark with huge eye lashes: they sort of reminded me of a new born calf. She was a maori girl, slim and petite, gentle and soft and she was a transmitter for love... and baby, I was receiving loud and clear!

She went by the absolutely glorious name of Leslie Pooha.

Fate had brought us together in beautiful forest country, the place and time is really quite irrelevant, the only thing that matters in this story is love – unadulterated love – and the pursuit of happiness.

Day in, day out we'd work together amidst the pines, Van Morrison cassettes filling the air with passionate expectations, Leslie's occasional glances sending me into wild heart palpitations. I just used to float around all day. I can't honestly remember my feet actually touching the ground at any stage. Love had rolled over me like a tidal wave.

I would have climbed the highest mountain just for one small sip of Leslie's bath water.

I'd done me nuts.

Old Leslie thought I was OK too, I reckon. When we talked she'd gaze into my eyes and the sweet melody of her voice would almost hypnotize me. If I had the facilities I would have bottled her farts then and there.

Leslie Pooha was an angel.

One day Leslie emerged out of a crisp early morning forest fog pressed the play button releasing Van Morrison and asked me if I would like to come over to her farmhouse for dinner that night. With Van's frequency of love playing in the background I said, "Oh yes", and she seemed to drift off back into the fog again. It was like a dream, a beautiful dream.

The stage was set, you didn't have to be Professor Ludwig von Drake to realize that. Tonight dinner, next week we'll start a family and live happily ever after, not a problem, the stage was pretty well set.

That day finally came to an end and off I took hittin' the showers and polishing up a bit. I made sure not to eat anything as I knew Leslie would probably cook something really special. So me and the old Holden headed out to Leslie's farmhouse running totally on love (and maybe just a little unleaded).

Not surprising I was pretty excited so I tipped a few beers down while I was making the miles to Leslie's farmhouse, probably a few too many actually. By the time I got there I think I was already a little stung.

Leslie was a gracious host topping my glass up with red and sending me into a spin with every smile that emanated from her beautiful little maori face.

Then came the meal. It was a pasta number. Leslie gave herself a little girly serving and then dumped about five kilos of it in front of me. So I ate the lot just to be polite. I mean, she could have served up a cow pat with a candle on it, I still would have scoffed it, just because it came from her kitchen.

To this day I reckon the meat was a bit raw but who knows, it could be an old maori tradition you never know. So, there I was, I'd had a heap of beer, red wine and a bucket full of raw mincey pasta swilling around in me guts and I was starting to really feel it.

We had a few more reds, then Leslie came out with a huge mug of this milky coffee. This was gunna test me out– I knew it.

I couldn't say no to Leslie, she was too precious. I would have drunk the coffee out of her dirty old sand shoe if that's what it came in. Me stomach started to really churn but I thought I had it covered. I was pretty confident I could see this one out. Somehow I finally got the coffee down but I could feel the perspiration starting to bead on my forehead.

Leslie was so sweet and caring as it was getting late she suggested I crash on the couch. Well it had been a nice night we both agreed. So Leslie gives me a blanket and bids goodnight casually radiating a smile then casually radiating away into her bedroom. She really was something else.

I laid down for ten minutes, I was feeling a little crook, a little pissed and a little disappointed. I thought I could have done a bit better. Maybe tried a bit of romance. Then that voice starts in my head, you know the one, the one that keeps telling you *'have a crack, have a crack, be cool, she's waiting – forget the couch, forget the couch, be brave, be brave, have a crack!'*

You know the voice. Surely I'm not the only one that ever hears it?

I resisted for a while but shit, I'm only mortal, I'm only flesh and blood. I was madly in love and I was convinced Leslie was waiting for me.

That was mistake number one.

Walking into Leslie's room I soon discovered a side to her personality I didn't know existed. She went off her rocker to put it mildly and after a truck load of abuse she spun me around and directed me straight out the door. Pronto. Bang went the door. It wasn't a goer! I don't think I even got a word in. *"Piss off back to the couch"*, I think were her actual words.

At this stage I couldn't really help but get the impression that romance was slowly going out of the evening.

Yep, slight miscalculation alright, could have happened to anyone. Next thing me stomach started to really pump, this time there was no stopping it. The 5 kilos of raw mincey pasta wanted out and it was gunna take the milky coffee and all the beer and red with it. They were all on the way up and there was no looking back.

It was gunna be a one way trip!

I must admit I panicked, it was dark and I didn't know the layout of the house. In a few seconds of sheer terror I couldn't find the toilet, couldn't find the back door. I was in more trouble than the early settlers.

It was gunna have to be the kitchen sink!

I just made it in time to assume the position ... and then my whole world exploded, kilos and kilos of it, I spewed like I'd never spewed before. It was commendable how I kept it confined to the sink, well I thought I did anyway.

Next thing was the clean up. Leslie hadn't fronted which meant she hadn't heard me reefing. That was a real stroke of luck. Now if only I can get rid of it I'm right.

There was a toothbrush next to the tap so I grabbed it and started pokin' all the chunky bits down the sink. No worries I'll sort this one out. Leslie won't know a thing. After a bit of this and a bit of that it looked pretty good. So back to the couch, the place where it all began, the place I should have never bloody left.

With the morning light came complete and inconceivable horror.

Leslie was up and she was wild, and I'm thinkin' the last time I seen a 'Haka' performed with so much conviction, was in the Rugby World Cup – and I don't really blame her either because the curtains that donned the window above the sink looked as if they'd been spray painted with vitamized pizza!

Another costly miscalculation on my behalf.

I staggered out to face the music and believe me it wasn't a choir of angels either. It was heavy metal with a twist and the twist was me getting the boot straight out the door.

"Piss bloody off."

And believe me, goodbye was not only all she wrote but she screamed it out at quite a high pitch as well – and you know, our relationship never quite recovered from this. Actually I can't remember her ever talking to me again.

Not long after that I left the forest, and drifted on. I'd totally blown it with the angel of love.

Somewhere down the track I heard on the grapevine she ended up with a Japanese golf course manager. Lady luck must have dealt him some good cards alright and he obviously played them a bit better that yours truly ...

Because I just couldn't take a bloody trick!

That could have happened to anyone!!

MUSIC HAS ALWAYS BEEN A PASSION FOR ME, no doubt about it. I picked the guitar up as a kid and learnt a few chords and as the years went on I suppose I developed my own style. I have written a few songs about different places and people, but mostly about emotional things, for example, women that have dumped me. You know the story, 'she tore my heart out and threw it out the car window, oh baby, baby'! Yeah... Deep and meaningful stuff. Emotional, moving stuff like, 'she twisted and she turned me, just like some kind of tool, poor fool, a love tool...' Pure poetry.

Vocally I have been described as Jimmy Hendrix on half a lung, but you know, as good as I was, I'd never really got anywhere, getting pissed and singing around the camp fire was my only claim to fame.

It was beautiful to see how I could work a drunken campfire crowd.

You know... I'd bring them up with an uplifting version of 'you only live once, then you are dead for a long time' (one I wrote based on fact), then I would take them down to the emotional basement with a devastatingly tear jerking version of 'Island Girl'. One I wrote about a Maori girl who invited me around to her farmhouse for dinner, and I got pissed and spewed up in her kitchen sink – yep, I really had evolved all right! I was accomplished. Probably one of the greatest camp fire singers of the post war era.

Usually I would be half shot, perched on an esky, singin' me guts out, it might be a stock camp or a bunch of tourists or just mates, but I always seemed to be the one entertaining.

When I was in full flight, I could do no wrong, like the time up at Kakadu, I was singing a deep and meaningful to a bunch of Germans around a campfire and unbeknown to me, my left ball was hanging out the side of my shorts.

I couldn't work out why everyone was staring. I thought they were checking out the painting on my guitar. Some of the women actually looked horrified! And I'm thinkin', 'shit... I know it's a sad song, but hey, it's not that bad.' Then the penny dropped, I looked down and seen one plum hangin' out, so I casually finished the song and said "old tradition folks, in Australia, we always sit around the camp fire with one ball hangin' out", and you know, they almost believed me. You see, when you have the crowd in the palm of your hands, you can get away with stuff like that.

Whichever way you look at it, in all modesty, I was a very polished performer, usually half pissed, but polished all the same.

Where does a bloke go to once he's reached the top of the heap? Lets face it, I'd written ten songs and I knew another two, so that made twelve songs, now that's what you call real depth. Creatively speaking, I was blossoming, and I could feel it deep down in my creative soul that something big was creatively just around the creative corner.

Now you wouldn't read about it, but three incredible twists of fate took place around that time. Events that would eventually lead me to my musical destiny. Let's go through it:

Twist of fate number one:

Whilst working as boat driver on the crocodile night adventure cruise on the Katherine river one night, I hit a floating log and an incredibly fat lady goes catapulting out of the boat, does three somersaults, goes into a half pike, levels out and spears straight into the black depths of the Katherine river. We fished her out but she was fairly distraught... understandable.

Twist of fate number two:

After filling out an incredibly long accident report concerning one lady, I flicked through the local paper and there it was – shining like a beacon in the job vacancy section: 'Singer Guitar Player Wanted in Outback Resort'.

Twist of fate number three:

I get the arse from Crocodile Night Adventure Cruises on the Katherine River. Now tell me that wasn't fate... Without a doubt, I was being guided by a higher force, there's no doubt about it, it was almost spooky.

My horoscope for the week said the sun would be in Uranus, but I was feeling that good, I wouldn't be surprised if the sun was shining directly out of it.

So on the phone I hop. I get straight onto the Manager of the Resort, and like any decent young Australian, I was prepared to spin any amount of bullshit I had to, to secure the job. Realizing I was being guided by a higher force, I approached it with a fair degree of confidence.

Now the Resort Manager answered and proceeded to fire a few questions at me. I pretty well had them covered, and when I told him I'd just returned from a tour in Memphis, he really started to get interested. I told him I knew all the oldies as well as the newies and was willing to bend over backwards and sing them directly out my arse if need be, he said "that probably wouldn't be necessary", but he liked my enthusiasm.

Well anyway I got the job.

So I packed the old Toyota for the trip and headed off... I was planning on about two to three days travelling, taking into account pubs along the way. I threw in a few extra flash shirts, you know, a couple of frilly rhinestone jobs for the gig, and I brushed the cobwebs off an old pack of condoms, just in case the impossible happened, and I blew out of Katherine trying to remember the words to an old Creedence song.

And I tell you what, there's nothing like the open road to unwind and do a bit of thinking. It's almost therapeutic. As usual I seemed to see the romantic side of things as opposed to the more realistic. I had visions of sipping cold beer by the resort pool in the day, and at night getting standing ovations for my twelve fantastic songs.

One thing for sure, I had just enough money to get there and that was it, so if it didn't work out, I was stuffed. But being the total optimist I am, thoughts of failure didn't enter my head.

The old Toyota just purred along the Stuart Highway, reliable as ever. Shame the rego had run out, but hey, 'you can't win them all' I'm thinkin', as I swerved to miss a wedge tail eagle that was chewin' on a bit of wallaby schnitzel squashed on the road.

I was ready to root, shoot and electrocute, ready to pour my heart out in song, ready to devour audiences with my charm, I was ready for the Sydney fuckin' Opera House, and no sweat, I had the rhinestone outfit to back me up. By the time I'd arrived at the Resort I was just a quivering mass of musical internal combustion on a hair trigger just waiting to go off.

So into the reception area I strode, a jukebox on legs looking for the Manager.

A nice little girl at the counter asked me if I would like to book a room for the night, I think she thought I was a tourist, I said, *"she's right I'm the new musician, gunna do a bit of playin."*

She took a double take and looked at me in disbelief. I said "hey baby, I don't look like much, but wait till I croon", she went red and just slinked away. I'm thinkin' what did she expect, bloody Elvis?

The Manager finally showed up. He was a skinny little bloke of about five foot two, he reminded me of Barney Rubble from The Flintstones. The Duty Manager was with him. He was deeply tanned and had a sharp look about him similar to the wedge tail I nearly run over on the way down.

They both looked me up and down as if I was the dingo that took Lindy Chamberlain's baby, and I'm starting to think I might be a late scratching.

Slowly and unsurely they greeted me, it was all very cool. I obviously wasn't what they expected, but we went through the motions. They showed me my room which was pretty good and gave me a book on rules and regulations whilst working at the Resort. It was just crammed with all sorts of laws and codes of behaviour, not what you'd describe as a little light reading. Actually it read more like the 'Old Testament'. It looked to me like they were running a pretty tight ship, but no problem, I reckon our paths shouldn't cross too many times.

I hung my rhinestone numbers on a coat hanger and went for a walk to check things out.

The resort was split in two sections, one section had a campground, some budget dormitories with a cafe and small bar. Plenty of people were milling around. This area was obviously for the backpackers and caravaners doing it on the cheap. The other section was more exclusive, luscious motel rooms, a fantastic restaurant and balcony area, a great pool, and nice bar. This area was obviously for people, packin' a little brass. Both areas had great views out across the flat. The colours and the general feeling of this area was tremendous, so much spirit.

The next morning I was up with the sun ready to create musical history. The butcher birds were going their hardest at first light outside my room, giving it heaps with their throaty little tunes. It was like they were trying to teach me a new song, but I'm thinkin', 'hey ... relax guys, I already know twelve.'

Then I checked out the rules and regs book and turned to the chapter concerning staff breakfasts. I moved off in the appropriate manner and walked to the appropriate eating area and appropriately ordered an appropriate staff breakfast, and in the manner appropriate of a staff member, I quite appropriately banged it down, then ripped out an incredibly appropriate fart which by the way wasn't in the rule book (unless it was in the small print).

All these rules were already giving me the shits; it made a bloke feel like he was back at school.

After breakfast, I figured it was time to chew the fat with Barney Rubble about my musical destiny, and as it turned out he wanted me to kick off that night on the balcony up at the flash restaurant.

Apparently, there was a little stage set up and a PA system already to go. I jokingly said to Barney "the girls better have both hands on their pants, because when I start strummin', emotions go wild." Barney Rubble just looked at me as if I was a complete imbecile. It was like I was speaking in a foreign language. To say we were from opposite sides of the track would have been an understatement. Different planets would have been more like it.

So later that night, I rocked up at the flash restaurant, ready to kick off a startling new career in music. Half of me was dead excited and rearin' to go, the other half (and I think probably the half with the brain in it), was thinkin' what the hell have I got myself into now.

The restaurant was pretty busy, probably about 100 to 120 punters and all pretty stylish types, some real knockouts just quietly, and I'm thinkin' 'there's more clam getting around here than the Barrier Reef', but I'd say they would be out of my league. But then again, stranger things have happened I told myself, trying to keep the old confidence up.

Now out on the balcony there was a fair few people sitting around, sipping champers, and watching the sunset, some had already put the nosebag on and were getting into it. Every now and then I'd catch a glimpse of Barney Rubble's Duty Manager flying around the restaurant like a Nazi Storm Trooper that just got wind there was a Jew around somewhere. No doubt about it, he was a hard case all right. I'm pretty sure if I caught fire he wouldn't have pissed on me to put me out.

Well, I thought, no time like the present, time to plug in and pour it out, time to slay them which the big twelve, time to give these dudes a musical education. It was destiny time.

So up to the stage I went, which by the way, was two old pallets with a bit of old carpet thrown on top that smelt like tom cat piss. They really outdid themselves with the stage. I'm thinkin' the PA system looked like something they stole from cash converters, but I plugged the old girl in and adjusted a few knobs, and to my surprise, the thing arced up, so I gave the guitar a couple of strums and it didn't sound half bad.

Then I did a quick test one two with the mike, and I was ready to fire.

At that moment I would have paid big money for a shot or two of rum just to settle me down a bit. But without further ado I said into the microphone, "*Gidday folks, my names Phil O'Brien, has anyone been to India? Well get this one intayu*" and off I went strumming the guts out of the guitar and singing me hardest. I reckon I sounded not bad at all, somewhere between Willie Nelson and Reg Lindsay. I was really croonin' it out, and as I finished off the first song I half expected a clap or two or at least a nod of a head. But there was nothing... No one even looked up... bugger all. So I said into the microphone, just to stir them up a bit, "*thanks folks, that was one I wrote back in Memphis with the King*" ... Still nothing. So off I went into song two, an emotional song about how women use me for my body. I finished that one and said "*thanks folks that one's doing big things for me in Zimbabwe*" ... still nothing.

So on I ploughed, song three, a tune about a German Girl that dumped me, called Waltzing Von Hilda ... still nothing. So I sang a couple more and then announced that I'd just take a short break. "*You've been a great audience*", I said ...no one gave a shit. I'm thinkin, either none of this mob speaks English, or they just couldn't give a 'flying fuck'.

I think I was pretty right on both counts.

As I walked up to the bar, I noticed most of the people were European, mostly German by the sounds of things, and with a sprinkling of Japanese thrown in, there was bugger all Australians. They probably couldn't afford the joint. Most of the punters were really tucking into the tucker as well, probably hungry after hiking around all day, so no need to take it too bad, I'm thinking. My next bracket might get a bit better response.

A cold beer would pick me up no doubt. So up to the bar I went, only to find staff aren't allowed to drink whilst on duty. Well I didn't need that, no way, that was a piece of tragic news, and if I wasn't depressed before, I was now!

I'm thinkin', 'this is getting crueler by the minute.'

But into it I went again, song after song, the only response I got this time was some old bloke walking past, flicked twenty cents into my guitar case. I didn't know whether to laugh or cry or get up and snot him.

The one positive thing about playing at this restaurant, was the fact I could sing pretty well anything. For example, you could play the same song a couple of times or even just make one up as you went along or sing the same verse over and over to kill a bit of time. As no one spoke English and no one gave a stuff, you could get away with anything. Of course you'd get the odd look from some of the staff at times, but they'd get over it.

Every now and then I'd con some German into getting me a beer and I'd go and drink it out in the car park, away from the other staff. Musically, I think I was going pretty good, and after a few weeks, I was kind of enjoying the experience.

Unfortunately my love life still hadn't really ignited and it was causing me concern. Night after night incredibly beautiful women

Phil O'Brien...
Should have stuck to playing around the campfire.

would file in and out of the joint and I think as far as they were concerned, I was just someone making noise in the corner. But you know, as bad as things get sometimes, you should never forget one thing... that 'every dog has his day' - well he's meant to anyway.

I remember it was a Saturday night. I know this because the night before was Friday the thirteenth, and a plague of giant beetles came through the resort.

I was playing out on the balcony at the time. Beetles were everywhere doing the big Kamikaze, so all the punters moved inside and the staff shut the big glass doors. That was quite OK, except for the fact they locked me out there playing to no one, and everyone inside the restaurant was looking out at me on the balcony like I was a nut. Covered in beetles, I was that pissed off, I just carried on regardless.

Finally, when Saturday night came, everyone was back on the balcony again and the beetles had moved on to wherever beetles move on to. I was strumming away when all of a sudden me top lip started curling back a bit like an excited old ram. Now this usually only means one thing. So I had a quick scan around and sure enough, there she was, sitting just to the left of my intricate stage set up, and she was on her lonesome. She definitely had all the right stuff in all the right places but for some reason she looked down in the dumps like someone had just run over her dog or something.

Now it had been quite a while between drinks for the old campfire singer, but the senses were still very finely tuned. She had boyfriend trouble written all over her face. Without a doubt a very vulnerable time for any impressionable young woman. I thought I'd strum a sad one and see how she took it.

She took it rough.

She slumped down on the table, head in her hands, I'm thinkin' 'this girl needs help', so I played a bit of an uplifting one, but it didn't seem to help. I think she was still too affected from the sad one I played before and she was going down fast.

Any minute it looked like she was just going to drop down on the ground and probably go into the foetal position.

'Shit! Better do something' I'm thinkin', so I announced to the Germans and Japanese, *"you've been great but I'm taking a short break"*, and as per usual they showed about as much emotion as a stack of fence posts laying at the railway station.

So I casually strolled over, you know, the responsible caring, human being I am and genuinely asked her how she was going. I was half expecting her to tell me to get lost, but she looked up and just gazed straight into my eyes, and for a minute there we just locked onto each others gaze like a pair of heat seeking missiles. I think she thought I was OK, which made me think shit, she's either hard up, fed up or just plain washed up, so we introduced ourselves, and I know it sounds ridiculous, but it was at that precise moment I realized... I was a bit on the bugle. This was due to the fact the last time I wore that shirt, was about six months ago when I was working in a stock camp near Borroloola and I hadn't washed it since.

She must have noticed the smell as well, and said, *"mmm, mmm, what's that aftershave you are wearing?"* "Ah", I said, "er, ah, it's a new one called, ah, it's called, 'Brumby'." *"Umm, very earthy"* she reckons, *"very earthy."*

Well, after that we just hit it off, and as I predicted, she'd just busted up with a bloke down in Melbourne, she sounded like she was doing it tough, so I told her a couple of my hard luck stories and it seemed to pick her up a bit.

We decided that we both needed a little bit of an adventure, and I came up with the great idea of going for a swim in this lovely little spring that was nearby. I'd never swum in it before, but it looked really inviting, I told her.

So we left the roaring crowd to dribble into their buffet and we took off.

It was a beautiful steamy hot night. Complete with wild lightning and the sounds of thunder rolling across the flat. It was as if nature had choreographed a perfect scenario for romance.

I felt pretty sure I'd be climbing into the saddle at some stage of the night, no worries at all.

'Every dog has his day', I'm thinkin', and after a little swim, it should be back to her $250 per night bungalow for a little bit of the business, no problems – put your money on the campfire singer because he will be running home strong in this one. It's a cert.

We got to the spring and peeled the gear off and jumped in. The atmosphere was incredible and pretty soon we were kissing and steaming up the spring, so I thought that I would get the momentum going a little more and give her a bit of the old caress. So I run my hand gently down her thigh, and I start feeling all these rubbery lumpy things all over her and I'm thinkin', 'shit, what's the go here'. Then it hit me, *leeches*! The spring was full of them. Unfortunately I had to tell her, we better get out. It was a real shame because she was getting up to maximum revs and I'm sure we were just about to consummate our relationship.

We got out and when she seen the leeches, she really chucked a wobbly, I mean she really lost it. I tried to get them off her as quick as I could, blood going everywhere, of course it looked worse than what it was. If you get them off quick, it's really no problem, but I couldn't seem to tell her that. She was going hysterical, screaming and stuff. She wound herself up that much, she started to hyperventilate, so I slapped her gently to try to snap her out of it.

Then she slapped me about seventeen times harder, grabbed her gear and stormed off. No problem, I'm thinking, 'every dog has his day' all right – but not this one!

Next night, I'm back on the balcony trying to put the trauma of the previous night behind me.

Feeling a little emotional, I had an idea for a new song. I was gunna call it 'The Lord giveth and the Lord taketh away'. So I strummed out what was in my head and as usual, the Germans and Japanese just grazed on. Then, out of the blue, races Barney Rubble with the

Duty Manager goose stepping along behind him. He must have been on leave from the Gestapo.

They came up to me in a fairly urgent manner and announced that a group over in the corner that were doing a tour with the bus company 'Australian Pacific' wanted me to come over and lead them off in a rousing Happy Birthday Australian Pacific, as it was the bus company's 70th year of service. Well, I thought for a minute and I said *"look mate, I'd do just about anything to help anyone, but I take my music pretty serious and I'll be buggered if I'm singing Happy Birthday to a bus."* Well, old Barney's bottom lip dropped and the look on his face reminded me of someone that had just lost everything in a bush fire. The little bloke was shattered. The Duty Manager on the other hand looked as if he was ready to clip two electrodes to my testicles and hit the switch.

They both spun on their heals and took off, and I realized I lost a lot of popularity over that one, but bugger 'em, I'm a serious artist, so I went back to singing the 'Lord giveth and the Lord taketh away', the story of a young bloke who misses out on scoring because of a violent leech attack. A very sad emotional little tune.

The next night up at the balcony, the most amazing thing happened. One of the punters came up and actually talked to me. He was a young German and he wanted to know if I could cook a damper. I said *"yeah, I've knocked out a few in my day."* He asked if I could show him how, I said *"no worries"*, so the next day, I organized to meet him.

He wasn't a bad sort of bloke, and when I caught up with him the following day, he had an esky full of cold cans. He definitely showed a lot of initiative for a German, so we took off in my old Toyota, I found a bit of good wood and proceeded to show him the ins and outs of damper creation.

We had a great day drinking an enormous amount of cold beer under a particularly hot sun and in the end rolling out a nice damper.

When we finally got back to the resort, I was fairly lubricated. The

German bloke had pretty well run his race and the last I seen of him, he was staggering off with the damper tucked under his arm. So I was thinking as I'd hardly eaten all day, a rum or two would be nice. You know, something with a little substance. I wandered into the little bar at the resort, no problem, as I was off duty. It was legal to have a drink. I thought I was moving pretty well for a bloke that had been drinking all day. I was feeling really happy with myself, life was good. I had been on the piss all day with a German, which in itself, was an international act of good will between our two countries. A fantastic effort. Now time for a little rumbo jumbo.

The bar manager, who by the way, was built like a Canadian brown bear, gave me the once over and just scowled. Although he had nothing on me, I could see he didn't like me much. I don't really know why, but he was wound up tight, that was for sure. I managed to get a rum out of him and then I started chatting with two extremely charming girls at the bar. Me being five eighths pissed, I was full of bravado, telling the girls all sorts of bullshit ... they were lapping it up and we had a good old time.

My excitement was short lived because they announced to me they were lesbians. But hey, that's OK. I said and so I asked the age old question that all Australian blokes have to ask in this situation... "*Is it OK if I watch?*"

The thing is, you've got to ask that. It's like buying a lottery ticket. You never expect to win, but then again you just might get lucky.

The two charming lesbians just laughed and said, "*no, not this time*", no worries, we had a good old laugh over that one.

Well it must have been too much for the performing Canadian brown bear bar manager, the three of us having a good time at the bar was really burning him up. It must have all got too much for him, so he came over and fronted me, and as I looked up at him, he demanded that I get out of the bar. No pleasantries or why's or reasons, just *GET OUT*, as if he was talking to someone's mongrel dog.

Well the old adage, 'the bigger they are the harder you fall', doesn't really apply when you've had a tank full and although I'm a peace loving person, I wasn't gunna stand for any of his stand over tactics, so I tried to grab him and give him one, he'd really got under my goat and I was gunna punch him somewhere into the next fortnight.

Some German backpackers jumped on me and tried to stop me, which was fair enough... they were just trying to defuse the situation. By that time, the 'bear' had picked up the phone and was ringing the boss Barney Rubble, so I grabbed the phone out of his hands and speared it straight at his head. He ducked and the phone smashed against the wall, exploding into a million pieces. I said *"ring him now, give him a ring now, see if he's home."* He was fairly stunned, so I took the opportunity to stand back and gloat.

The moment was short lived, because, little did I know, his wife was in an office at the side of the bar and she'd rung the boss. Before I knew it, there's Barney Rubble in his pyjamas, standing right next to me.

So, the show was over. He wanted me in the office first thing in the morning, so I left the bar peacefully, as I really don't like violence, but I suppose everyone's got limits to what they put up with.

The next morning I went to the office with a hangover that would have registered on someone's Richter scale. There was me, Barney Rubble and the Duty Manager, dying to tear my toenails out one by one. I'm sure he would have loved to stake me out over an ant's nest.

Barney reckoned *"you've damaged resort equipment, I'm going to have to terminate your contract."* Then he reckoned, "you also refused to sing Happy Birthday to Australian Pacific and I'm sure you weren't going to sing Jingle Bells at Christmas and no doubt you would refuse to sing Auld Lang Syne at New Years Eve." "Well", I said, "mate, I think you've got me on that one" (I mean how can you argue with that.) This was no place for a bloke with my artistic capabilities, so I got up, packed up and pissed off.

The last I seen of that Resort and my musical destiny, was in my rear vision mirror – slowly disappearing.

An hour or so down the road, I stopped to boil the billy and make some coffee as the hang over was getting the better of me. I pulled off the road and lit a fire and got some water going. I plucked out my guitar and had a bit of a strum. Through my hangover haze, I realized one thing, the old campfire singer was back where he belonged... just singing around the campfire!

Never turn your back on a leech...

A Gob-full of Tobacco Slime

PJ AND PEG WERE MIDDLE AGED American tourists I chanced to meet while I was doin' a tourist run out to the 'Bungle Bungles' in Western Australia. Me and about twelve people headed out for a 3-day trip. And old PJ's sittin' up next to me in the 4-wheel drive bus type vehicle I was drivin'. Now he's chewin' away on this tobacco stuff and he's holdin' a cup and he's chewin' and spittin' and dribblin' this black shit into this cup as we're drivin'. He'd chew a bit then he'd have a dribble and drop a big black globule of tobacco slime into the cup... and I'm thinkin', 'shit, this is makin' me feel crook!'

All PJ's teeth were stained black from this stuff and he'd smile away tellin' me stories from the United States ...hoiken and spittin' and chewin' and about every ten miles his cup would be full so he'd tip it out the window and start again.

Most of this black stuff was ending up down the side of the bus.

But off he'd go.

He reminded me of an old dairy cow gettin' stuck into a bit of good cud.

Well, anyway around the camp PJ was no different, but he didn't worry about the cup, he was just hoiken and drippin' these dirty black globule hangers all around where people were eating and camping – It was rugged stuff.

Late one afternoon after a bit of a hike we hit this waterhole that was still full from the wet season rains and old PJ jumps in and all of a sudden he starts to squirm around and bob up and down and he looks like he's in all sorts of trouble. He starts yellin' and wavin' and I'm thinkin', 'shit, he's gunna drown'. So I dived in and swam over and old PJ's really havin' a big panic – but there was nothin' wrong with him, he'd just jumped in and then realised he had his chewing tobacco in his back pocket and he didn't want it to get wet. So he was trying to hold it out of the water with one hand and tread water with the other – but he wasn't having much success. So I rescued the chewin' tobacco and I'm thinkin'...'what next?' PJ clambers to the bank and his black toothed smile creeps back across his face as he's reunited with his chewing tobacco. Old PJ was havin' the time of his life, smiling away with his black teeth, drooling and gaggin' and drippin'.

Well on the last day of the trip PJ's lovely wife, 'Bobbi-Sue' decides to light up a smoke – it was the first cigarette I'd seen her with the whole trip and unlike PJ, Bobbi-Sue was very reserved and absolutely no trouble at all. When PJ see's Bobbi light up, he flies right into her and bores it right up her!

He reckons: "*Gard damn Bobbi-Sue, that's a filthy habit*" – and he tears shreds off her for lightin' one up. No-one could believe it, the whole group were totally gob smacked and I'm thinkin', 'shit PJ – fair suck of the sauce bottle!'

NOW TRYING TO CATCH CROCS AT NIGHT isn't something you do for a bit of fun... it's not like having a few coldies on the beach, or watching the cricket... you know, it's a fairly serious way to spend an evening. But there I was, doin' my duty as a croc farmer, tryin' to build up a bit of breeding stock. And I can honestly say there's usually two things you constantly think of when you're poking around in a little dingy up some black tepid, shitty swamp looking for a croc. Firstly you wish you had a bigger boat, and secondly, you wish you were a long way away doin' something else. To a bloke that wasn't born on the courageous side of the tracks, it's pretty hairy stuff.

Finding them is one thing, getting them tied up and in the boat... well that's another, but you seem to get through it and along the way you really have some interesting experiences and not only that, you meet some bloody interesting crocodiles. None more than a particular croc we called Ben Hur and like the movie production of the same name... Ben Hur was big!

He wasn't only big but hell he was agro.

I mean he really had a bad streak runnin' through his cold blooded dinosaur veins.

I'd say with my modest experience on crocs, Ben, if he hadn't eaten anyone already, would definitely be the type of croc that would take someone, if given half a chance. I know it took a few years off my life tryin' to tie the scaly big prick up.

So after the joy of getting him tied up and into the tinny and the laugh a minute fun time getting him from the tinny to the croc farm ute, there was only one more carefully calculated intricate part of the operation left, and that was the drive-in bottle shop – you know, none of us guys would have won any medals for bravery – I mean, time to give the old nervous system a bit of a stabilizer.

Unfortunately Ben Hur was too big for the ute and his tail was hangin' out the back which scared the shit out of the bottle shop attendant. Ben Hur was already making a name for himself around town...

Back at the farm as with any croc we caught I measured him and sexed him just for the records. Sexing a croc is quite an interesting procedure. You have to stick your finger fair up the croc's clacker. Now this always gets a reaction out of the croc. Of course you only do this while it's securely tied up.

But big Ben Hur was all male, there was no doubt about it.

We released him into a natural billabong area at the back of the farm. There were several other crocs in there as well and it had a good solid fence going around it. Right from the start Ben Hur just didn't take to captivity at all and to show his resentment he went on a rampage, virtually killing half of every living thing down there.

Ben Hur was completely out of control.

No croc was safe, he was on a wild killing spree. And after about a week the once quiet picturesque natural billabong area of the farm resembled the killing floor at Katherine Meatworks. There was bone and guts laying around everywhere. There was no stopping him.

We went out spotlighting again and caught another croc in the bay, we had to, I mean we needed to get the numbers back up. But Ben's killfest continued and next day the new croc was just a headless corpse floating belly up in the once tranquil billabong.

Somehow we had to stop this holocaust, but I'll be buggered if I knew how. As quick as we were catching them, he was dismantling them. Of course there was the odd suggestion of shooting him right between the eyes, but as tempting as that sounded it wouldn't work because Ben was just too bloody cunning. You only had to go anywhere near the billabong and he'd duck under the water and you wouldn't know where he was. He pretty well had us euchred.

When all hope seemed lost the most amazing thing happened. Ben Hur decided to pull a stunt that could only be described as bloody spectacular. Whether he had it planned or it was just off the cuff, no-one will ever know.

During the night Ben crawled out of the billabong and made his way across to the fence and ate a hole in it big enough to drive a car through. He then marched into another pen that held three crocs, a big male called Wally Gator and two females, Laverne and Shirley. Ben flogged the hell out of Wally then he hunted the two females back through the hole he ate in the fence, and on to the billabong,

Obviously Ben was in the mood for love.

The next morning me and the boys turned up for work and thought we'd check on the latest carnage down at the billabong.

We were stunned...

One of the females Ben had busted out the night before, Laverne, was sunning herself on the bank, and there's Ben just bobbing around in front of her, butter wouldn't melt in his jaws, swimming up and down like a love sick pup. He'd do some funny manoeuvre then look around at her, then some other funny manoeuvre then look back, just to make sure she was watching.

He was gone, he was love struck. He wasn't interested in the other female Shirley, just Laverne. She was the one for him.

We examined the hole in the fence and saw Wally Gator layin' there, bark off him everywhere, he was in a bad way. The tracks in the sand told the whole story, where Ben come up from the billabong – the eating of the fence ... the fight ... then taking Laverne and Shirley back to the billabong. Pretty romantic stuff for a crocodile.

Actually it reminded me of an Elvis movie, you know Elvis meets girl, beats up existing boyfriend, wins over girl... sweet.

I'm thinkin' there was a definite parallel with Ben's performance. Croc meets croc, mauls male croc, then takes up with female croc. But when you look at it Ben had it all over Elvis because he not only won the babe... he ate the fence!

Not even Elvis at his romantic best pulled something like that out the bag.

So there it was Ben Hur doing it for love.

Honestly speaking Ben never hurt another croc again while I was at the farm. He underwent a complete personality change. He put it all behind him, he'd settled down. Not only did he dote on her constantly but when it was feeding time the big test for any croc, he'd let her eat first then Ben would nibble away at the scraps... he'd actually gone pretty soppy.

That just goes to show you the power of love, doesn't it? This was genuine stuff. This was a love affair jam packed with emotion, chivalry, adventure and total commitment. Probably one of the greatest love stories of modern day, and I felt honoured to have

Top: 'Ben Hur'. Before he did his nuts
Bottom: After he did his nuts

played a small part... well anyway, this is the way I figured the whole thing...

But you know – no-one would ever suspect a croc could be capable of love, no way, not in this day of scientific rationalities. You ask any expert, crocs don't have emotions – they don't care – they're just instinctive killing machines.

But Ben was the exception I reckon... and I don't care what any expert says – I'm positive – that lizard did his nuts!

Laverne & Shirley...
Players in a wild crocodile love triangle

MANY MOONS AGO I WAS WORKIN' in a stock-camp at a place out towards the Northern Territory, Queensland border. It was hard country out there, and it attracted some pretty hard type characters as well. Everyone had a story to tell, you know, they were either on the run from the law, their wife had left them, they'd lost everything gambling, become an alcoholic, had a breakdown or different combinations – like: their wife had run off and they lost everything gambling – you know... everyone had a story.

The camp cook we had was no different. 'Scabie Jack's' wife and three kids had left him and as a result he'd turned himself into a chronic alcoholic. Every now and again the Alice Springs cops would run him out of town, so Scabie Jack would get a job cookin' in a stock camp somewhere, tryin' to dry out.

He really wasn't much of a cook but he was a humourous sort of bloke. He got the name Scabie because of a habit he had of always rubbing and scratching at different parts of his anatomy, mainly his backside. He wore his hair like Elvis slicked right back and he had the big sideburns to match, not a lot of teeth, and for a particularly skinny bloke, he had a huge pot guts.

Jack had developed his own way of speaking as well, substituting nine out of ten words with either 'the caper' or 'the turnout'. For example: you might come in for dinner and say "What have we got, Jack?" and he'd reply something along the lines of *"Ah, bloody run out of the caper so I'm bangin' out a bit of the turnout..."* After awhile you sort of got to understand him a bit.

Out bush he was meant to be dryin' out but often his craving for grog would get the better of him, but because there was none around, that didn't stop him... he'd make his own.

One little number he called 'Scabie de Monte' was a combination of lemon essence and after shave lotion. Another one of his specialities off the top shelf was boiled down 'Nugget' boot polish and beetroot juice. I'd heard rendering down boot polish was pretty common for alchies in the bush but Jack's claim to fame was that he knew the secret process of getting all the lumps out. So he'd have a few nips of this stuff to keep him going in between whipping up culinary delights.

Jack's menu starting from Saturday was stew everyday till the following Saturday, and it wasn't a different stew either, it was the same stew, he'd just top it up everyday. But on Sunday it was his special dish. He'd tip a tin of 'Keens Curry Powder' into the week old percolating stew and make the big announcement... *"Curry tonight boys... she's a big one tonight, bit of the old turnout..."* As if it was a real treat! Actually, relatively speaking... it was!

But all the same everyone liked Scabie Jack, he had a real sense of humour.

One time these two jillaroos came up from down south to work in the stock camp, they were pretty green. The first day they asked Jack where do they go to the toilet. Of course, there wasn't one but Jack just kicks the top off an old anthill and reckons, *"Give that a bit of the old turnout."* The girls had no idea how to take him.

But the outback life suited old Scabie and his funny ways and it was always a laugh with him around.

Back in town Jack had his share of run-ins with the police as well. On one occasion Jack had been on the piss all day at the Stuart Arms and then decided to get a taxi home. So he staggered to the taxi rank but all the taxi drivers there refused to take him because of his drunken state.

So Scabie Jack wants to fight them all.

Next minute the cops arrive and they are all real chummy chummy. "How ya goin' Jack?" they reckon, "Jump in, we'll give you a ride home."

Well Jack thinks this is great, so he gives the taxi boys the fingers and jumps in with the cops, and they take off.

Pretty soon Jack works out they're goin' in the wrong direction.

"What's the caper, what's the caper?" he reckons. Next minute they pull up at the Hospital. *"Hey my joint's not around here. This ain't the turnout."* Next thing they got him inside... 'And what's this tube for?' Jack's thinkin'.

Well anyway they pumped his stomach out, poor bugger. I think the cops were just tryin' to teach him a lesson.

Yeah, old Jack had his share of ups and downs that's for sure.

Another hard case at that property was the boss, Big Bad Bert, and he was one tough bastard. Anyone with half a brain never crossed him because Bert didn't mind swingin' a few and it didn't take much for him to crank up. If Bert reckoned the sky was falling you'd agree, and reckon' you'd seen a bit of it come down as well. This is just how it was.

Bert was a huge bloke and a good cattleman but for some reason the horse he used to ride was very small, just a pony. Bert's feet used to nearly drag on the ground. It looked particularly funny but shit –

you'd never even think about laughing - he'd kill you, nothing surer.

He had a wife and two kids and I don't think the kids had ever been to town. One day I walked past the homestead and at that time I had a real bushy beard. Well... the little boy reckons *"Hey Mummy there goes God..."* The kid just didn't know any better.

Bert used to spend a lot of time around the homestead and he'd only come out to the mustering camp every now and again to check things out.

I remember one night we'd got a call on the two-way he was comin' out. Well everyone knew he was a crazy driver as well.

The year before he'd run someone over in their swag while they were asleep.

So there was about 10 of us huddled behind this big tree in our swags, hopefully avoiding getting run over when Bert roars in, in his Toyota.

Sure enough you can hear him comin' for miles off, and you can see the dust rising nearly filtering out the moon. And Bert screams in and hits the skids, shit goin' everywhere... and he's got his high beams pointed at all us blokes huddled together in our swags behind the trunk of this big tree.

And we all look up and Bert bellows out – *"What's wrong with all you Bastards, you scared of the dark or something...!"*

Well the replies went along the lines of: *"Yeah Bert, always have been"* ... *"Never did like it Bert"* ... *"Bloody oath Bert"* – I mean no-one told him we were just tryin' to avoid gettin' run over because he was a mug driver!

One young bloke in the camp Bert sacked one time, I'm not sure what for, but Bert, as with a lot of those managers on remote properties had a light aircraft and flew the young bloke back to the Alice.

Somewhere along the line the young bloke must have given Bert some cheek because after they landed at Alice Springs Airport, Bert knocked the young bloke out, flew off and left him laying on the tarmac out cold!

The air traffic controllers had to get someone to drag him off as there was an Ansett plane about to come in.

Lookin' back I ended up staying out on that place a little longer than I would have liked to, but like a lot of the other blokes ... I think I was just too scared to quit.

U P IN KATHERINE ONE TIME I HAD the good fortune to make the acquaintance of a young bloke named Steph Johansen, and like myself he shared a real passion for music. Steph's chosen instrument was the bass guitar and he knew about 3-4 notes on it. So me being able to play approximately three chords on the guitar meant we really hit it off, and many an afternoon was spent strummin' and pluckin'.

Now as it quite often happens mates drift on and over the years you lose touch with each other. I'd heard on the grapevine Steph settled in Adelaide, so as I was heading down that way to visit family one time, I thought I'd look him up.

I don't mind the odd burst in the big smoke. It's always an adventure, and providing you don't stay too long it's quite enjoyable.

So I managed to track old Steph down, and I was rapt to find music was still a big part of his life. We had a few coldies, as you do, and caught up and Steph proudly announced he'd formed a little rock 'n' roll band. He reckoned they'd been practising hard for some time now and they finally had a few gigs lined up at a few pubs around town. Things really looked good.

But then Steph breaks down and tells me... things did look good – well - that is, up to about a week ago he reckons.

Poor old Steph's face drooped as he told me the tragic story how the guitarist had taken off with the drummer's girlfriend... and disappeared. *"Oh well... that's rock 'n' roll,"* mumbled Steph, starin' out into space like a bloke that had lost everything. *"And we were meant to be playing this weekend, but it looks like we're shot now..."* sobs poor old Steph.

Then his face seems to brighten up again and I could see the cogs were turning, and a cheeky smile starts to creep across his face and he reckons: *"Not necessarily. Not bloody necessarily old mate,"* and I'm thinkin' ...'Oh shit'... two beers later and you guessed it:

I'm in the fucking band.

It's just a small pub he reckons, and don't worry we got two days to practise. *"It'll be great fun"* he reckons, makin' it all sound just dandy. "You'll probably end up pullin' a root... *This is rock and roll my old mate"* he reckons ..."*You're dealing with rock and fucking roll."*

The next couple of days were spent at Steph's flat practising with the drummer. Most of the songs were early rock 'n' roll and not too hard to play so they lent me an old electric guitar and away we went. Steph really was living the rock 'n' roll life – you know – the only thing in the fridge was beer, the only herb in the kitchen was Pot and all anyone ate was pizza, and when the music got too loud the neighbours would throw rocks on the roof – it was rock 'n' roll.

The first little show Steph had lined up came around pretty quick and before I knew it, we're settin' up the gear in a pub in Adelaide and I'm thinkin' 'you know it should be fun, a few people would probably turn up... bit of a sing-along, a few coldies.' Well a few people turned up alright – the joint was packed – every down and outer in Adelaide must have been there. Then a biker club rocks up and a couple of blokes ride their bikes into the pub and the place is really hottin' up.

Steph had obviously spread the word and I'm thinkin'... 'This isn't just gunna be a few strums in the bar – it's shapin' up more like friggin' 'Woodstock'.'

So in they jammed, and she was a rough old crowd.... I mean the women had just as many tattoos as the blokes and I think everyone was smokin' a pack an hour judging by the haze. A bloke just about needed a bloody snorkel. So Steph decides it was time to play, and that was OK by me because I think the safest place to be was probably the stage!

Now it wasn't long after we started playin', maybe the third of fourth song, a fight breaks out in the crowd, and before long, the whole place is fighting. Everyone. I mean everyone!

There was blokes fighting blokes, women fighting blokes, and women fighting each other. It was well and truly on.

Just like in the movies the band tried to play on but the fight spilled over onto the stage and it was every man for himself. Chairs were flyin', glasses were getting smashed – they were jabbin', gougin', bitin', kickin' – and that's just the women.

I looked across at Steph. He'd draped himself over his amplifier like a fire blanket tryin' to protect it while the fight raged all around. I was wrestling with one bloke and I'm thinkin' of all the dangerous things I've done in my life but playin' in Steph's band has gotta be up there with the hairiest.

The shit was hitting the fan. One bloke had torn off some guttering from out the back and was trying to ram it into what looked like one of the bar staff. Some young girl leapt off the stage and landed on his back, and just clung on like a baby koala.

It was a real 'shit fight'.

I never thought I'd ever be glad to hear the wail of a police siren, but I was that time.

So the cops file in and start dragging people out. The bar was pretty well trashed. I couldn't believe it. What happened to the couple of coldies and a sing-along? I felt sorry for Steph. He'd put a lot of work into this, but the show was over, that's for sure.

The cops finally emptied the place, which just left us to pack our gear up, and the bar staff who were still sweepin' up glass and tryin' to tidy up what was left.

The poor old hotel manager was just standing there in the middle of the bar – stunned.

Now as if all this wasn't enough drama for one night, Steph goes and lets his blue heeler dog out of the car, and the dog runs straight into the bar, runs straight up to the feet of the hotel manager and chews the shit out of a cigarette lighter laying there. The lighter blows up, burns all the fur off the dog's head and starts the carpet burning. All around the feet of the manager is on fire and the poor bugger's tryin' to stamp it out, and the dog's running around yelping and carrying on... his head smokin'.

If I didn't see it I would not have believed it – unbelievable.

So Steph helped put it out, and the manager who must have been Italian holds his arms up, looks at the ceiling and screams – "*Why-a ...Why-a you bringa so mucha trouble to my-a hotella ... Why-a ... Why-a you bringa the trouble ... Why-a?*"

But Steph, ever the optimist reckons: "Any chance of another gig?" And I'm thinkin' '... probably a bit of bad timing with that one Steph.'

Well, the old Italian looked down at Steph, slowly ran his hand through his greying hair, and quietly and calmly said: "*Take the dogga and the instrumento and getta losta.*"

I'm thinkin' whoever wrote that line 'It's a long way to the top if you wanna rock and roll' really hit the nail on the head ... that's for sure.

So on the way home there's me, Steph and the dog drivin' along, and Steph reckons: *"Don't worry mate. We're playin' down the Port tomorrow night."* "Gunna be a big one" he reckoned, *"gunna be huge!"*

I'm thinkin', 'oh great ... I can hardly wait.'

Next night we're settin' up at this pub down Port Adelaide way and Steph to his credit wanted to really make this night a real winner. So he hired this lighting guy to come down and do some fancy lighting while we rock and rolled, you know, give it a bit of atmosphere. Well this in theory was a good idea, but the lighting guy turns up pissed as a lizard – I mean he could hardly walk. So we set up our gear and then helped the pissed lighting guy to set his lights up ... then the lighting guy curls up and goes to sleep on the floor. He was proving a really good investment.

A few people wandered in, so we start playin' and believe it or not things were goin' really good, the few people that turned up really were getting into it, no trouble so far. It was going good.

Well anyway we were into our second bracket and no one had even thrown a chair. But I had this feeling it was just too good to be true, and unfortunately, that feeling proved correct because late in the second bracket the lighting guy regained consciousness and went up to the bar, and when he thought no one was looking he tried to steal the money out of the till. Now this guy was all class. He gets caught, the publican rings the police, the police come and because they've associated this guy with the band ... we all get kicked out, and there was no third bracket – we got the shunt.

So there's me, Steph and the dog drivin' home, and poor Steph can't believe it. "But don't worry. Tomorrow night's gunna be great", he reckons ... tryin' to look on the bright side. *"This pub's in a really nice part of town, great mob out there. We'll go down well ... I've really been looking forward to this one ... We'll shit it in"*, he reckons.

Well me and the dog looked at each other, and for a moment there I could swear I seen the dog shake his head slightly from side to side ... but no ... he couldn't have ... surely not.

Next night we're settin' up and Steph was right. It was a nice place and it was in a nice part of town but while we were playing some not so nice person stole the St Vincent de Paul poor box from the bar. Well somehow along the line we got blamed because of our now increasing bad reputation. So once again the night was cut short, and we were asked to pack up – I couldn't believe it!

This one really hurt Steph. A bloke can only take so much, and on the way home me, the dog and Steph never really spoke much – spirits were pretty low. I felt for Steph. It was OK for me. I mean, it was all an adventure, but Steph had put a lot into this rock 'n' roll stuff ... and you couldn't help but think he really was havin' a bad run of luck.

So Steph went and did what most rock 'n' rollers do when things aren't going too good. He went home, drank all the beer in the fridge ... smoked all the herb in the kitchen ... and ordered a pizza.

But Steph had guts and he wasn't gunna be beaten, and a few days later he's ringin' me up and was ready to fire again. He was makin' a come back.

This time he had it all worked out ... *"no worries, shit it in"*, he reckons ... *"we're gunna shit it in"*, then he's yellin in the phone: *"Rock and fucking roll ... You're dealing with rock and ultra fucking roll!"* It took him a while but when he actually got around to giving me the facts it didn't sound too bad. He'd got onto a pub in the Adelaide Hills who were willing to give us a go out in their beer garden. Well this sounded good. It was more my style, layback beer garden scene in the hills ... it should be fun. I mean what could possibly happen?

So there we go, me, Steph, the drummer and the dog rock up to the Hills pub, and everyone wants to know what happened to the dog's head. So we told the story and everyone cracked up.

And I'm thinkin' 'this is great.' 'You know you can't beat country people. They'll give anyone a fair go. It seemed we'd found our niche – no worries, this will be great.' Then I take a squiz outside at the beer garden, and the beer garden's on a 45 degree angle. You see the pub was on top of a hill and the beer garden which was probably an after thought was actually the side of the hill, but with a few chairs and tables scattered around.

So there we are set up and we start playin', and we're playin' on a 45 degree angle and everyone's dancin' on a 45 degree angle.

Now playin' on a 45 degree angle wasn't really a problem. I mean it was different but as long as you kept your footing it was OK. The drummer had his drums tied down to some tent pegs someone lent us.

Steph reckoned . . . "Any band can play on the flat, but you gotta be good to play on a 45 degree angle."

Well that's all well and good but on top of all this, something was wrong with the pub's electrical wiring, and I mean it was serious. You'd put your mouth near the microphone to sing and an electrical arc would jump from the microphone to your lips. I think it was an earth problem, but shit it give you a good ol' boot! And after a while the old lips started to really feel it. Steph who was doing most of the singing copped it bad. His lips had swollen right up and he looked like Daffy Duck.

It was a wild old show playin' on the side of a hill getting electrocuted. But Steph seemed to take it in his stride. I think pain and suffering was all part of the rock 'n' roll life and a real rock 'n' roller has got to have a bit of a burden to bear or else it just wouldn't be right.

So by rock 'n 'roll standards this gig was a huge success. Nothing got stolen, smashed or broken.

On the way home Steph couldn't be happier and of course he reckoned this is only the beginning and nothing was gunna stop us now. Who knows where it's all going to end because we're on a roll he reckoned – *And that's Rock and fucking roll,*" he's yellin'. I looked around at the dog and I could swear I seen his eyes roll back in their sockets as Steph launched into another Gospel according to rock 'n' roll.

Well anyway it made a change from the bush life, that's for sure, and whichever way you cared to look at it, it definitely wasn't boring.

I got a phone call from Steph midweek. He'd punched the drummer out, something to do with a girl. Well anyway in true rock 'n' roll fashion, the band looked like it had self-destructed. I was sad to say it was the end of an era, and even though the era only lasted about two weeks I won't be forgetting it in a hurry, that's for sure.

Steph couldn't talk long. He was heading out to get a drum machine ... He had it all worked out. He was changin' his name to 'Texas T Bone' and buyin' a cowboy hat. *"Yi-har,"* he's yellin' in the phone. *"Yi fucking har,"* he reckoned. *"Country's where it's at ... big market out there. Yi-har,"* he's yellin. *"Gunna shit it in! Got it worked out!"*

"Anyway old mate how much longer you stickin' around for?" Steph's asking. *"Maybe we can just get together and ..."*

You Can't Hide in a Glasshouse.

T HE WET SEASON IN THE TOP END stretches from roughly Christmas to Easter, so because of the heavy falls of rain at that time, things out bush go a bit quiet. Roads get washed out, creeks and rivers rise. It's really no time to be travellin' around. So because of the conditions it can be a bit hard to find work at that time of the year.

The idea's to save up during the dry and then just sit out the wet – in theory that works great, but when you're like me, a totally unorganised, irresponsible, financial disaster, the wet season can be a pretty lean time, and believe me, I've had the seats out of the car looking for loose change on more that one occasion.

But you know life's a very fickle thing ... more ins and outs than a blue movie. I'm thinkin' one day you got cream in your coffee and next day you're resoaking your old tea-bags, if you get my drift.

The go is, you've got to grab hold of the opportunities that come your way and hold on tight ... seize the moment ... be responsible ... plan for the future, you know virtually all the things I don't ever seem to pull off.

The perfect example of my lack of all the above, is the time I got offered a job at a very prestigious national park. It was only for the wet season because some bloke was on long service, but it could lead to a full time position they reckoned. Well I jumped at it.

It paid well, great conditions, chance of advancement and not only that but you get to wear this real deadly national parks and wildlife uniform, with badges and logos hangin' off it everywhere. There was a career here for the taking, a chance to put my past behind me and become a responsible citizen, maybe even get a tax file number ... you never know. This was my one big break and I was gunna hold on tight. No way was I gunna stuff this one up as I had done so many times before with other jobs, this was different. I was in for the long haul!

They started me off at what they called the 'Entry Station', a flash new structure with these really stylish glass walls. The Entry Station was situated so as the tourists drove into the park, they had to pull up there. I'd take their entry fees and then give them maps and stuff and help them plan their trip.

As I was the first thing they saw as they came into the park it was important to present myself well, and really turn on the old professional attitude – the park being a World Heritage area and all. The tourists, mainly overseas visitors really expected a high standard of service, of which I could fake, no problems at all.

I was set like the proverbial ... jelly in a jam tin!

Things were going shit hot. The Entry Station was really decked out well, it had two air cons, a fridge, a microwave, a phone, it was paradise. Actually I wasn't meant to be sleeping in there as well but it was heaps more comfortable than the busted ass caravan I was meant to be stayin' in. And after all who was to know.

This was proving to be an all time great wet season ... meeting all sorts of tourists ... making good money ... wearing a riproaring uniform and soaking up some great aircon. I'd never had it so good – well that was until I met these Irish girls...

A van pulls in with four Irish girls and they had good time written all over their pretty Irish faces. So I did the entry fee and the map thing. Then we started rappin' away and they reckon after work meet them down at their camp for a drink.

I'm thinkin', how much better is life gunna get? Shit.. it can't get much better. Surely not.

So after work I cruised down to their camp and slipped right into it. As with most Irish people I've met, they were very charming, and a lot of fun. One drink led to about seventeen and the last thing I remember I was playing a penny whistle doing an Irish jig around the fire – pissed out me brain.

I think I finally headed back to the Entry station about three or four in the morning – fully marinated.

Then horror struck ... as it sometimes does.

The next morning I woke up to about thirty Germans banging on the glass walls of the Entry station ... and there's me, no clothes on at all, choked down on top of me swag. I must have slept though the alarm!

There was no hiding because the joint was all glass.

They had their faces pressed up against it, some of them had even started taking photos. In full view I somehow got me shorts on and went over and slid the door open ... and I was lookin' rough. No shirt, no shoes, staggerin' around like I had Mad Cow disease ... I was in the horrors, penny whistles still playing in me brain. The Germans were probably wondering if they had the right address.

I was shot to pieces. I had a hangover that would have killed a Shetland pony but I took their money and threw a few maps around ... but the Germans didn't know what the hell was going on and as the coach driver ushered them back on the bus I heard him say: "Interesting wildlife around here isn't it folks." "*Yar ... Yar ...*" they reckoned "*...Yar ... Yar.*"

Needless to say, I never got asked back to work there again.

My temporary position that was to turn into a full-time position had suddenly gone from temporary to 'Thanks for comin'.'

I'd blown another one...

OLD TERRITORY SAYING...

Never get mixed up with an Irish Girl and a Pennywhistle...

IT WAS GETTING TOUGH on the old Croc farm, pet meat prices were slipping higher and higher, and the crocs seemed to be eating more and more. Things were starting to look a little tight. All the hatchlings, which were the saleable item, were growing out really well, but they weren't quite ready to sell just yet. So cash flow was on the lean side. I figured it might be a good idea to do a bit of hunting and try and save the farm some money.

I wanted to target water buffalo as they weighed in at over a ton and that meant a lot of meat for the farm. Roos and feral pigs weren't much good, too much effort for not a lot of return. So we needed to get amongst a few buff and we'd be out of the immediate shit.

Water buffalo aren't native to Australia. They were introduced back in the late 1800's, but they adapted so well they virtually reached plague proportions causing enormous erosion and damage to the wetland areas of the Top End of the Territory. So the government launched a huge eradication program in the 1980's to try and wipe them out. They were almost successful, but there was the odd area where buff could still be found.

The thing was, getting organized enough to get out there and get amongst them.

Unfortunately at the time the aboriginal workforce on the farm were away as there was a big ceremony on, and I didn't know when they'd be back. I needed a little help, so I thought it was a pretty good time to go visit an old friend of mine, Colin Powell.

Powelly was a part aboriginal bloke in his fifties, a top bushman and his skill with a butcher's knife was legendary and he was a good bloke to have around. These days he lived a relatively quiet existence, but in his early days I think he played it pretty hard. One time a few years back he rattled someone's cage a bit too hard. I don't know the exact circumstances, but Powelly got shot twice in the stomach at point blank. Somehow he survived it.

He always joked that before he got shot he had a serious diabetes problem, but after he got his pancreas blown out, hey, it really wasn't a problem anymore. He was a happy go lucky kinda bloke, and I really liked him.

I drove down to his camp in the early morning. Powelly had just finished breakfast. Breakfast that day consisted of a 6 pack of beer and one half roasted echidna. A true breakfast of champions! Iron man stuff. The only thing Powelly liked better than echidna was tongue, he loved tongue, bullock tongue, buffalo tongue, any tongue. He'd boil it up and slice into it like cheese. 'Better than chocolate', he reckoned.

A cold beer and a slice of tongue and Powelly was happy. He was in his twilight years and was really enjoying the finer things in life.

Powelly had some good ideas where I might find a mob of buffalo, and with a little luck he reckoned we just might get a few in the freezer.

The place he suggested was about 7-8 hours drive away out towards some open coastal plain, a fair hike – but that was where they were he reckoned. So that was good enough for me, and as I hoped Powelly was dying to come along as well. He reckoned he hadn't had a good feed of tongue for ages. And someone better come and show the young bloke how to do it.

How could you argue with that, Powelly had mileage and I respected him for it. Next move, a couple more blokes, a couple of rifles, a trailer, some diesel and no self respecting buffalo in East Arnhem land would be safe.

The next friend I called on was Tony Pierce, one of my close friends, a middle aged bloke, he ran the local slipway where he did repairs on boats. Tony was a real Errol Flynn style character. Nothing fazed Tony and he was only too happy to come and help knock a few buff over for the Croc farm. He thought it might be a good chance to bring his son Jimmy on a little adventure, show him a few of the old man's tricks.

Mark Johnson was the next mate I grabbed, an easy going bloke, very resilient, Mark only had to eat every second or third day and like the drover's dog, was all prick and ribs.

So all up she was a pretty star studded line up.

Together we managed to scrape up an old World War II, three-o-three rifle off some old digger and one .22 Magnum. The .22 would have been great for rabbits but no way would it ever stop a buffalo, but we brought it anyway as not to offend the old bloke that lent it to us.

Next morning we met at the Croc farm, it reminded me of that line from the famous poem, 'Man from Snowy River', the bit that reads:

'*All the cracks had gathered to the fray*'... What a joke!

Everyone hungover to the shit house after a blinder at the local club the night before. I almost called it off, but the meat situation was just too desperate.

Powelly hadn't fronted, so we drove down to his camp and we found him there still a little under the weather from the night before, but his enthusiasm was undaunted. So we loaded him into the back of the Toyota and hit the track. Me and Jimmy in the front with Tony, Mark and old Powelly flaked out in the back of the tray-back.

It wasn't long before there was grumbling coming from the back. Apparently Powelly in his sleep was squeezing out these greasy oily 'Echidna farts' and they were kind of eddy-ing around in the back, causing a little grief for the other blokes.

I forged on as we had a long way to go, every now and again you could here the sounds of someone dry retching above the road noise.

It was shaping up as 'one of those trips.'

After a few hours on the Central Arnhem Highway (which by the way is just a dirt road with a big name), we turned off onto a little goat track, that hopefully would take us out to the country Powelly was talking about. It was a slow old trip through creeks and wash aways, and up and down rocky hills and gullies. The hangover heads in the back were starting to call out for the 'hair of the dog' so we had a bit of a blow in the shade alongside a pretty little creek, so we all relaxed with a cold beer.

The Crack Buff Hunting Outfit wasn't lookin' real flash at that stage. We looked fairly average actually, but after a few pick me ups we'd level out, I was thinkin'. So after smoko we crossed the creek and pushed on, the track petering out until there wasn't one. Through the bush we poked and as Powelly predicted the country started to open up and just as the sun was setting we found our-selves on some promising looking open plains country.

A little bit of buff shit was dotted around the place and the odd pad – so the signs looked good. The Crack Buff Hunting Party had got over their hangovers by now and were slipping into the beer a bit, but I was confident everyone could still handle themselves – they were just enjoying the trip.

No doubt we would have sent a chill down the spine of any buff that night as we stalked the open plains. We were knife edge sharp – like a crack military unit! It may have looked like we were driving around in circles stopping every two minutes for someone to have a leak. But in actual fact, we were like a venomous snake, just waiting to strike!

When the sun was well and truly down we arced up the spotlight. Around we went, spotlight sweeping, following tracks and keeping a sharp eye out.

Senses finely tuned...

Powelly was asleep and Jimmy was nodding off and not much noise coming from the back either... it was quiet confidence – 'thank God the beer had run out', I'm thinkin'. Great mates but shit they can drink piss!

Then presto; one buff caught in the beam of the spotlight, totally mesmerized about a hundred metres away... *"Righto Tony, Mark go for it! Buff!... There go for it."* Nothing seemed to happen, then Powelly woke up and instinctively screamed out, "SHOOT THE BASTARD."

At last, action on the back of the Toyota, ca-lang clang, beer cans kicked out the way, bullets being dropped by shakey hands, another beer can goes rattling around. The boys on the back weren't real slick. By now the buffalo's long gone. So finally someone gets a shot away but, forget it... the buff's not there anymore.

Well we wouldn't have won any gold medals for that performance, I'm thinkin'. Time for a bit of a meeting.

We all got out and had a bit of a walk around, and splashed a bit of water on our faces, had a leak and the Crack Buff Hunting Team did a bit of soul searching. We psyched ourselves up for a better effort next time. I pointed out it had been a great trip getting out there but now we've got to get into it a bit, make things worthwhile.

No worries, the Crack Squad were in agreeance, we were on a mission.

So off we poked, this time in a much more alert state... well at least everyone was awake this time! We scanned and scanned with the spotlight then bingo... two shapes moving across the flat up in front of us, kaboom went the fire power from the back of the Toyota, kaboom and the two shapes kept hopping out across the flat. It was two roos, but it didn't matter, we'd missed them anyway.

Shit, I'm thinkin', it's gunna be one hell of a long night.

One hour later, I must admit, I was just about to think we weren't gunna do much good, then, bang, coming around a bit of a bend we hit the jackpot... about six or seven buff out on the flat. No way were we gunna miss this mob so I booted the Toyota and raced off across the flat. I wanted to get around them and work them into a bunch. Then I figured we might have a chance of getting the lot.

Easier said than done.

The buff were up and running but we were gaining, the ground was rough and bumpy and the blokes on the back were hangin' on for dear life but no one had started to abuse me yet, so I knew everything was all right.

Across the flat we roared in the old Toyota, we finally caught the mob and I swung out wide and rung around them pushing them into a small group. The boys started shooting and I kept driving in large circles around the buffalo keeping them together. The crack shots on the back were going their hardest but it's never easy shooting from a moving vehicle and it was pretty rough country, a little pot-holey. The buff decided it was time to make a break for it, at this stage we'd dropped a couple and wounded a couple and about three galloped off so we took after them and managed to pull alongside one and shoot it. Then we tried it with another one and somehow Tony missed and managed to shoot the indicator light off the Toyota!

I thought we'd steady up for a bit so we went back and put the two wounded ones out of their misery. That was five and we figured that would do us. The plan was to get stuck into it at first light and cut them up and try to get the meat back to the Croc farm freezer before it went off.

The Crack Buff Hunting Outfit was now starting to tire a bit. It had been a big day and we'd done pretty well considering it only took about three hundred and twenty seven bullets to get five buffalo... but there'd be plenty of beef for the Croc farm. Time to roll out the swag and rest up for the morning.

As I was laying in my swag that night I had a little laugh to myself. It was quite ironic but not all that far away from where we were, was one of those Safari-type camps where big game hunters fly out from the USA and stuff and pay thousands of dollars to nail a buff.

'Shit', I'm thinkin' 'a couple of them could have come with us for nothing. They would've had more fun anyway.' I couldn't really work out why people pay all that money to kill animals. Personally I hate killing anything but the old buffalo causes a lot of damage and it's a feral animal and this time the meat was sure going to a good cause.

First light came around pretty quick as it usually does when you're really stuffed and the Crack Unit was a bit sluggish getting out of their swags, but after a billy of tea and a bit of steak, the Outfit started to step pretty lively. It was gunna take a big effort to get these buff cut up. We knew we had to really move it as the weather was pretty warm and humid, just the right conditions for sending meat off in a hurry.

Powelly was an absolute artist with a knife, he dabbed and poked and sliced like a real Picasso, it was great to see him in action. With a knife in his hand, old Powelly was transformed, he wasn't Powelly anymore, he was Powelly van Gogh, ready to create another master piece. He'd look at it from this angle, then from that angle, a slice here, a poke there, next minute the hind quarter's off, a lick with the steel, a dab, a thrust, then the shoulder's off, a quick jab or two and the tongue's out ... A true artist.

We finished the first two and by then the sun was up and it was getting warm so we started to rush the next couple, Powelly as artis-

Jimmy, Powelly and the author...
The crack buff hunting outfit prepares to strike

tic as he was, was puffing out, so I went at it a bit harder and made a slip and sliced the side of my hand open. It was a pretty bad cut, plenty of blood coming out, so I wrapped a rag around it, the bleeding eventually stopped, but it slowed me right down. Not long after that Tony sticks a knife fair in his leg just behind his knee, he'd somehow slipped and drove it right in. He went down big time. Apart from the bleeding he went into a bit of shock as well, so we wrapped a blanket around him and laid him in the shade.

The Crack Buffalo Hunting Outfit was looking a little rag tag, we were going down like nine pins, but we kept at it – the sun getting higher and higher.

The trailer was finally loaded with the last hind quarter. Tony needed stitches pretty badly so we wasted no time and headed off, Powelly complaining he never had time to boil a tongue up!

It was a slow old trip back with the trailer full of buff meat, poor Tony wrapped in a blanket bouncing around on the back, Powelly craving a cold beer and a hot tongue, and me trying to negotiate the goat track towing three or four ton and with a hand that didn't want to stop bleeding. It was a real slog.

We got back to town just on dark. The morale of the Crack Buff Squad had deteriorated slightly after the 8 hour trip, everyone including me was absolutely stuffed. As we pulled into the hospital I'll be buggered, because there's a water buffalo feeding on the lawn just out the front of Emergency. I mean you wouldn't read about it!

The sophisticated Crack Buff Hunting Fraternity were completely stunned, no-none even had the energy to throw a rock at it. Looking back ... I think we were all to exhausted to laugh, but we sure as shit laughed about it later.

After everyone got stitched up, I dropped Powelly and his bag of tongues off, he wasn't feeling too crash hot. I thanked him for his help and he wandered off to his camp tired but happy he had the chance to get out there and do a bit of hunting again – No-one ever expected this was to be Powelly's last trip.

Powelly the Artist in action

A little later down the track Powelly passed away and the Northern Territory lost one of its great bush characters. A hard life had finally caught up with him.

As a show of respect for Powelly we all agreed if we ever see that buffalo on the lawn of the hospital again we'll knock it over and bone it out right there on the spot, just for old time sake – he would have liked that.

SOMETIMES I WISH I HAD A DOLLAR for every interesting character I've met in a bush pub. I reckon I'd be rollin' in it... You know, I've seen all sorts of sights over the years wandering around the country... some real entertaining stuff, like the Driller and his wife that were on the piss at a little pub in the Kimberley – she lets go with a huge spew right in the middle of the bar, and while it's still steamin' he gets down on his hands and knees and laps it up and then looks up at her and reckons "*more salt bitch*" ... I'll never forget that. Events like that tend to stay with you a long time.

Another bloke I knew just to prove he never suffered from stage fright, used to pull his old fella out and urinate on the bar while staring the barman in the eye and ordering a beer. I've seen blokes eat glass, I've seen blokes stand on their head and try and skull yard glasses – with no trousers on. You know feats of amazing strength like the dwarf that climbed onto a bar stool tapped this big bloke on the shoulder and then knocked him out.

But one bloke that I'll never forget was this gnarly wrinkled up old Thursday Islander that used to drift into this pub from time to time. The only thing I ever heard him say was 'Number 9'. That was it! Just 'No 9'. He'd either just sidle up next to you at the bar and say 'No 9' or else he'd come in and rip out some really loud bird call, then everyone would turn around to see what was going on. There would be the old bloke and he'd just say 'No 9'.

Another thing he used to do once he'd got everyone's attention, was to light a match and then place it in between the wrinkles on his forehead and then put a cigarette in his mouth and using no hands, with his huge lips, he'd some how point the cigarette up to the match that was lit wedged in between the wrinkles of his forehead and light it. Then still with no hands he'd take a few drags and swallow it... swallow the smoke. Of course by now everyone would be looking at him so he'd make the announcement ...'No 9'. Then somehow he'd cough and next minute out of his mouth comes the lit cigarette still smoking and no-one can believe it. Then he'd reckon very solemnly ...'No 9'.

Don't ask me why but apart from the loud screeching bird calls he did, all that came out of his mouth was 'No 9', but in his own way he was a likable sort of bloke. You could talk to him alright, and he'd sit there and listen and you could talk about work or fishing or anything but the reply would always be the same... just 'No 9'.

I never found out why – no-one seemed to know, but he never seemed to upset anyone, he just did his thing.

The Australian bush sure seems to produce some eccentric characters alright. Moving around as I do going from job to job and place to place I suppose you end up taking a lot for granted, and things that other people might find a bit left of centre seem to merge into every day stuff for me nowadays.

Like awhile back I'm havin' a quiet beer and 'Number 9's doin' his thing on one side of me and on the other side is a bloke talking to an imaginary parrot on his shoulder ... and the scary thing is ... it all seemed so normal!

STORIES TO COME IN VOLUME II IN THE SERIES 1o1 ADVENTURES THAT HAVE GOT ME ABSOLUTELY NOWHERE"

THE STORY OF A MAN NAMED RAY
They picked on him as a kid – but Ray went bush... grew up... got tough and came back... and now he's got hold of a local phone book and he's beatin' up the town – in alphabetical order!

THE SNAKE LADY
Two hours in the Katherine Hot Springs with the Snake Lady... and life has never been the same since!

HOLY MACKEREL
Phil gets a job on a fishing boat – and every living thing in the sea wants to kill him. Phil almost finds himself getting buried at sea!

TEQUILA SLAMMED
Thrills and spills after Phil O'Brien wins a cash raffle and spends the lot on 'tequila'... things get messy!

THE CRICKET CARNIVAL
Phil represents his state in cricket but that's not all. Her name was Kim Lu and her mother thought she was working at a Chinese Takeaway... but Phil was dining in. A cricket story with a twist!

CROCODILE NIGHT ADVENTURE
Phil skippers a boat on the Katherine River taking tourists up and down at night. Wild times, crocs... drunks... women and the odd accident... or three!

DRINK WAITER BLUES – A SHORT STORY
Phil says 'fuck' and gets the sack (after ten minutes) – no long service owing in this one!

A GOOD WAY NOT TO START A BUSINESS
Phil starts his own camping safari business but after a swashbuckling first tour goes broke straight off... he doesn't win any tourism awards for this one

STORIES TO COME IN VOLUME II :

HOLY MACKEREL!!

ON SAFARI...

*Anyone know where the
Toyota is?*

*This is the South End
of a
North Bound Book...*